# Curating in a Time of Ecological Crisis

I0462062

*Curating in a Time of Ecological Crisis* reaffirms the relevance and impactful role of art, revealing how contemporary art exhibitions can capture the zeitgeist and advance new and collaborative approaches to a more sustainable inhabitation of Earth.

The book is largely focused on biennales, which it argues are the contemporary exhibition models with the greatest capacity to offer new perspectives and propose alternative ways of connecting with our social and natural environments. Felicity Fenner demonstrates this by showing how curators of these high-profile exhibitions are responding in creative and engaging ways to the issues that preoccupy artists and society more broadly, of which the ecological crisis is paramount. Drawing on case studies from different parts of the world, the author reveals how biennales can make a constructive contribution to debates and attitudes around climate change, and how the role of the curator has evolved to re-embrace a duty of care not just to art but to the natural world as well.

*Curating in a Time of Ecological Crisis* investigates how large-scale exhibitions of contemporary international art can become agents of change. As such, the book will be essential reading for scholars, students, and practitioners with an interest in exhibitions, curating, contemporary art, and environmental sustainability.

**Felicity Fenner** is a curator based at the University of New South Wales (UNSW), Australia, where she leads postgraduate programmes in curatorial and biennale studies. She is Chair of the City of Sydney's Public Art Advisory Panel and for over two decades has curated many exhibitions of international contemporary art, including for Australia at the Venice Biennale and for the Perth Festival. Her current research into the placemaking function of public art expands on the findings of her last book *Running the City: Why Public Art Matters* (2017).

# Curating in a Time of Ecological Crisis
Biennales as Agents of Change

**Felicity Fenner**

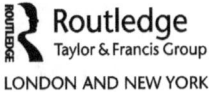
Routledge
Taylor & Francis Group

LONDON AND NEW YORK

First published 2022
by Routledge
4 Park Square, Milton Park, Abingdon, Oxon OX14 4RN

and by Routledge
605 Third Avenue, New York, NY 10158

*Routledge is an imprint of the Taylor & Francis Group, an informa business*

© 2022 Felicity Fenner

The right of Felicity Fenner to be identified as author of this work has been asserted in accordance with sections 77 and 78 of the Copyright, Designs and Patents Act 1988.

*British Library Cataloguing-in-Publication Data*
A catalogue record for this book is available from the British Library

*Library of Congress Cataloging-in-Publication Data*
A catalog record for this book has been requested

ISBN: 978-0-367-67192-1 (hbk)
ISBN: 978-0-367-67275-1 (pbk)
ISBN: 978-1-003-13057-4 (ebk)

DOI: 10.4324/9781003130574

Typeset in Times New Roman
by Apex CoVantage, LLC

# Contents

# Figures

# Preface

In late 2019 I left Australia during an unprecedented bushfire disaster and arrived in Venice as floodwaters rose to a 53-year high. It was difficult to rationalise the relevance of an art biennale when confronted with the immediate and disturbing evidence of climate change in opposite ends of the world in the very same week. Just a few months after the flooding forced the early closure of many exhibition venues across Venice, the Biennale of Sydney in my home city was the first of many major art exhibitions around the world to be suspended, postponed, or cancelled, this time due to the COVID-19 pandemic.

Artists are well positioned to comment on current issues and have done so for millennia, but I wondered what the role is now for curators. How can curators, especially those with jurisdiction over major exhibitions such as international biennales, make a meaningful contribution to addressing today's many environmental challenges?

This question led me to investigate those biennales already forging new models in response to the ecological crisis currently unfolding as a result of climate change. In the following chapters I have assessed the curatorial approaches of recent biennales largely focused on environmental challenges, collating the research in a way that will hopefully be useful in building capacity among curators to move from a model of presenting *art as inspiration* to one that proactively *inspires action*.

There are other biennales besides these that are committed to addressing environmental concerns, but the ones here have done or are doing so as a declared priority or core mission. Also, not wanting to rely entirely on secondary research, these are all biennales of which I have first-hand experience, for the most part including the specific editions discussed here. (Note: throughout, 'biennale' is used as an umbrella term to encompass recurrent international contemporary art events that in addition to biennials include triennials and the quinquennial documenta.)

Many thanks to my colleagues at The University of New South Wales (UNSW Sydney), Commissioning Editor at Routledge Books Heidi Lowther, editor John Mahony, editorial assistant Manas Roy and project manager Aruna Rajendran.

Without artists and curators there would be no biennales: thank you to my many artist friends and collaborators who have inspired this book and to the curators leading the way, including those who agreed to be interviewed for this research.

I am grateful for the support of my artist partner, who has shown me over the years that even if art cannot change the world, it can certainly be provocative. My perspectives on art and exhibitions are enriched by the company of my frequent biennale buddies and youthful sounding boards, George and Oscar, who together with their generational peers affirm my optimism that we can turn this ship around.

# Introduction

Imagine if it was inscribed in the governance of the Museum of Modern Art (MOMA), the Mori Art Museum, or Tate Modern that the chief curator and their curatorial staff be appointed for a maximum two-year term on a single-vision agenda. They do not have the luxury of working on long lead exhibitions that require years of research and planning. Instead, they must perpetually hit the ground running with a shovel-ready concept that captures the zeitgeist, ensuring the resultant exhibition genuinely conveys the preoccupations of contemporary artists and holds relevance for a broad range of audiences. This is the framework within which biennale curators work. As a result, compelled to deliver their vision within a short and clearly defined period, like politicians in their final term of office, curators of biennales are often much less risk averse than their tenured museum-based counterparts. Their biennale is their chance to make a statement or even make change. While this model empowers individualistic curatorial approaches, it also thwarts capacity building at an organisational level.

*Curating in a Time of Ecological Crisis* investigates how the world's most ubiquitous and high-profile contemporary art exhibitions – biennales – are addressing the major challenges of our time – climate change. The book proposes that in order to maximise their impact, biennales require a new paradigm, one that emphasises continuity between editions over bi-annual renewal. The existing model involves reinventing a biennale's thematic and curatorial premise every two years, which is an approach that has defined the unique agility and contemporaneity of biennale exhibitions. However, the book argues, it is no longer a model able to effectively support a growing sense of responsibility in biennale organisations to address the most urgent global issues, of which the ecological crisis is paramount.

The year 2020 was a line-in-the-sand year for humankind. In the wake of the first major health pandemic in living memory to impact almost the entire world population, many aspects of contemporary life are being reassessed, from the social and political to the commercial, industrial and cultural.

DOI: 10.4324/9781003130574-1

The COVID-19 pandemic has provided a chance to reflect and reassess biennale culture. *Curating in a Time of Ecological Crisis* makes a case for the relevance of art and exhibitions in the face of climate change. Harnessing the groundswell of environmental activism prior to the pandemic, the book analyses the capacity of contemporary biennales in particular to make a positive contribution to sustainability discourse. It reveals how biennales can not only embody the moment but can advance new and collaborative models for a more empathic and gentle inhabitation of the Earth. Its focus is on the role of the curator as an instigator and facilitator of environmental art projects with real-life application, invoking the original meaning of 'curator', a term that comes from the Latin 'curare' – to care or to cure.

Biennales differ from other exhibitions in their fast turnaround time and intrinsic capacity to respond to the issues of the hour in which each iteration is produced. Unlike museum exhibitions with long lead times, biennales are nimble, attuned, and responsive to the prevailing conditions. At a lecture in Sydney soon after her appointment as artistic director of the 2008 Biennale of Sydney, Carolyn Christov-Bakargiev spoke with characteristic candour of the need to turbo-charge her curatorial effort given the fleeting window she was afforded to deliver her ambitious, multigenerational exhibition.[1] In an interview for this research over a decade later, Christov-Bakargiev reiterated that the role of a biennale curator is inherently brief, necessitating a willingness to be agile with a radar attuned to artworks that will together make an exhibition that is meaningful in that particular place and time.[2]

Bruce Altshuler traces the establishment of biennales as the most socially relevant exhibition genre back to Harald Szeemann's documenta 5, which abandoned curatorial methodologies based on nationality, materiality, or typology in favour of a thematic approach that captured artists' preoccupations at the time. According to Altshuler, the 1972 documenta "established the model of the ambitious thematic exhibition assembled to order and interpret artworks according to a grand curatorial conception".[3] In the light of a neoliberal framing of art as superfluous to the core issues faced by governments today – evidenced by the diminishment of government funding for the arts as a sadly predictable response to unforeseen expenditure due to COVID-19 – this book examines recent biennale exhibitions from different parts of the world to reveal their important role as both vehicles of information and agents of change.

Because biennales occur with such pace and regularity, not since the world wars of the 20th century stopped the Venice Biennale has there been an opportunity to step off the treadmill of biennale planning, delivery, and consumption. In their introduction to *Curating in the 21st Century*, Wade et al. propose in the context of exhibition-making that we should only have a conference when there is a crisis because otherwise we are just chatting.[4] At this time of ecological crisis, biennales are the conferences of contemporary art. In contrast to the curatorial methodology of biennales over the last three decades – based on the model of a single curatorial voice deploying the exhibition format to illustrate a theoretical concept or theme – there is now a marked shift towards multilayered collaborations between teams of co-curators and between the biennale and its stakeholders. This book examines recent key biennale exhibitions that reject the positioning of biennales as elitist platforms for authorial singularity and visual spectacle, favouring a new model based on collaboration, education, and new restorative relations with natural environments and communities.

A dominant curatorial methodology in the new wave of biennales is the harnessing of local, traditional knowledge and resources for the purpose of remediating and revitalising environments and communities. Multibiennale curator Hou Hanru defines a biennale as "a space in which creative forms of global – local negotiations take place. It is through this engagement that the Biennial itself will obtain new energy and significance."[5]

The biennales here have found "new energy and significance" by embedding artistic and in some cases production activities in communities. The book reveals that while this curatorial approach has in part evolved in response to the emergence of socially engaged art over the last two decades, as chronicled in Bourriaud's *Relational Aesthetics*, the primary catalyst for the "healing" imperative that underpins many of the new biennales is environmental and social crisis. Notably, many of the new wave of biennales are committed to legacy building, an approach pioneered by the Echigo-Tsumari Triennale in Japan since 2000.

Leading by example, artists and curators in recent years have sought new approaches and methodologies that re-invest art and exhibitions with meaningful purpose. There has been a raft of exhibitions – including biennales – addressing environmental issues. The following chapters compare those curatorial models that aim to generate art and produce knowledge across areas of specialist research and consider how the role of curators has evolved to meet the changing expectations of consumers of art. In pandemic parlance, it explores how biennale curators, already by definition the most agile in our profession, have "pivoted" in response to climate change.

Flooding, catastrophic bushfires, and pandemics all have origins in the human activity that has changed the way our planet works. The "one-in-100-year" natural disasters of previous centuries are now so ubiquitous that we risk becoming desensitised to the severity of their threats to our survival. It has also become too easy to turn a blind eye to the plight of some people and places. Many smaller nations have already for years been hit by cyclones and sea level rises, yet their fate tends to fly under the radar of the world's media. Given our proximity and cultural connections to Pacific nations such as Fiji and Tonga, in Australia we are more cognisant than in the Northern Hemisphere of the impact of climate change on populations already suffering its worst effects (though not cooperative in trying to reduce them). This awareness has been boosted by biennales in the region, including Sydney's, with the recent inclusion of an impactful performative-based work by Latai Taumoepeau. A highlight of the 2020 Biennale, it provided searing insight into the issue of sea level rises in the Pacific and subsequently gained international recognition.[6]

In the world's wealthier nations, mainstream media coverage of "unusual" climate events has become disturbingly commonplace. The shocking footage of Australia's 2019–2020 bushfires and the resultant loss of precious ecosystems was mirrored in the west of the United States and along Mediterranean coastlines in 2021. In news footage more akin to apocalyptic horror movies than reportage, we watched fleeing residents and holiday-makers being herded into ferries ahead of approaching flames or forced to shelter on beaches. At the same time, deadly floods in Germany, Japan, and Turkey, soaring temperatures in Britain, heatwaves across Europe and tornadoes in North America drove home the reality of climate change to millions. Eventually, as the economically powerful nations could no longer deny the impending ecological crisis, financial and industry leaders began to respond with updated economic forecasts and insurance advice, but with very little vision in terms of remediating our crippling ecologies for long-term survival. While the much-anticipated COP26 climate summit agreed some ambitious emission reduction targets, the world still remains off track to counter the climate crisis.

Artists, in contrast, have for over 50 years been leading advocates of environmental sustainability, as outlined here in the context of museum and public gallery exhibitions in the first chapter. Today, it is the globally connected biennale events that are evolving to meet the challenge. Other biennales have in the recent past been launched in reaction to other world crises. Evelyne Jouanno's *Emergency Biennale in Chechnya*, for example, was in 2005 assembled to draw attention to the plight of people during the Chechen wars and more broadly to human and social emergencies caused by unrest and globalisation. In 2007, Prospect, New Orleans' biennale, also grew out of catastrophe, in that case Hurricane Katrina. Other biennales, already established as recurrent events, have in the past quickly changed course in response to natural disasters in their home cities: in 2013, Japan's Aichi Triennial and New Zealand's former SCAPE Public Art Christchurch Biennial, for example, both commissioned artworks responding to the major earthquakes that had recently devastated each of their cities.

The Chechnya and New Orleans biennales were initiated by a desire on the part of their curators to respond to humanitarian and natural disasters.

Elsewhere, in the past biennales have also been launched as platforms of resistance to the western bias of major biennales. The biennales of Havana (since 1984), Dakar (1990), and Yogjakarta (2011), for example, are dedicated exclusively to art from Latin America, Africa, Asia, and Oceania – the Global South. The sense of urgency underpinning the birth of these biennales has been instrumental in modelling discursive curatorial approaches to current biennales. As Claire Doherty observed back in 2007:

> Given that the places of the biennial have been reconsidered as points of exchange and collision, remade through intersections of social, economic and political relations, it is not surprising that the predominant forms to emerge from these context-specific invitations are social, spatial and interdisciplinary.[7]

Today, it is a given that curators of biennales approach them as "a discursive form, as an expansive event involving much more than the viewing of artworks", a model set in motion by Catherine David's "generative" documenta X in 1997 and expanded upon by Okwui Enwezor with the "platform" events of documenta 11.[8] A generation later, it is today painfully clear that the world needs to find ways to survive the present challenges, ameliorate their most painful effects, and learn to thrive in new conditions. Exhibitions and cultural institutions can play an important part. According to the 2022 Istanbul Biennial team:

> Art organizations all around the world face urgent, existential questions – questions of survival and relevance, about how they operate, for whom, and to what ends – biennials are not immune. . . . Art can refresh the vocabularies of public discourse, it can open new pathways of thought at a time of acute and complex planetary crisis.[9]

Given their high-profile platform, biennales are not only "not immune" to reimagining their raison d'etre but also well positioned to be leaders in forging new curatorial models. This is not to discount the contribution to environmental discourse made by individual artists and curators working outside the exhibition context, many of whom have successfully shifted perceptions of environmental challenges in recent years by advancing new, less exploitative ways of thinking about our interactions with the natural environment. These include those initiated by Cape Farewell since 2001 and until recently by the Centre for Contemporary Art and the Natural World in Devon (both UK), Lauren Bon's Metabolic Studio in California, Ou Ning's Bishan Project in China, Kamin Lertchaiprasert and Rirkrit

Tiravanija's Land Foundation in Thailand, and many individual artist projects in the C3West programme in Western Sydney, delivered under the auspices of the Museum of Contemporary Art (since 2007). Many of these projects, past and present, are captured in the Curating Cities database of eco-sustainable art.[10]

Environmental scientist Tim Flannery agrees that art can be a useful weapon in raising awareness and possibly inspiring action against climate change. In an art–science forum in 2020 he spoke of the need to bring emotions into the dialogue as scientific data and political rhetoric in themselves are dry, partisan, and potentially disengaging. Flannery argues that "now we have proven that climate change is real, we have to stop being rational and start being emotional", a quality that makes Flannery's own writing on the climate crisis so accessible and widely read.[11] This pursuit of an emotive response is echoed in the way in which many biennales are promoted as immersive, fluid, and provocative experiences, in contrast to more traditional exhibitions constrained politically or physically by museum infrastructures. Chris McAuliffe has noted in relation to biennales that "Canny organisers amplify these emotional effects with unusual venues (abandoned factories are a favourite), hands-on and interactive artworks, and the placement of striking sculptures or installations in familiar public spaces".[12] This has been a phenomenon of major exhibitions for decades, with "advanced artists and progressive curators" using such spaces since the 1960s.[13] Recent biennales with overarching themes around social and environmental sustainability have had less need for emotive backdrops, their audiences already emotionally engaged with – or enraged by – the topics at hand.[14]

Since the earliest times, art has been deployed as a vehicle of learning and knowledge transfer. In the late 15th-century Italy, Dominican Fra Michele da Carcano explained in a sermon the didactic and emotive power of images. Substituting his original references to the bible with words applicable to today's ecological crisis, it is clear that art can assume a similarly relevant role in contemporary times:

> Images of the Virgin and the Saint [natural environment] were introduced for three reasons. First, on account of the ignorance of simple people [climate skeptics], so that those who are not able to read the scriptures [science] can yet learn by seeing the Sacraments [evidence] of our salvation [damnation] and faith in pictures. Second, images were introduced on account of our emotional sluggishness so that men who are not aroused to devotion when they hear about the histories [ecosystems] of the Saints [nature] may at least be moved when they see them. . . . Third, images were introduced because many people cannot

retain in their memories what they hear, but they do remember if they see images.[15]

All the arts – literature, music, the performing, and visual arts – have the power to invest even the most challenging subject matter with emotive urgency. Large exhibitions including biennales, in contrast to small and solo art projects, often need to maintain audience engagement for a longer duration. This can be testing for curators, bringing together several artworks by a range of practitioners, as just one work based on unconvincing grounds potentially compromises the rhetorical value of the entire exhibition. Unless underpinned by scientific truth, art that addresses failing natural ecosystems, as an example pertinent to this book, risks being dismissed as either sentimental or sensationalist.

When it comes to large group exhibitions, the challenges of conveying meaningful messages about climate change in the pursuit of achieving greater awareness and possibly behaviour change in audiences are doubly problematic. First, audience expectation needs to be shifted. The popular and stubbornly persistent idea of art exhibitions as a form of passively consumed spectacle and entertainment can hamper intellectual engagement. As Shwetal Patel and co-authors assert in their biennale 'manual':

> We want to produce art, not institutions, to exchange, not transmit. And, if biennales are to 'matter' (to continue to recur materially, and to be of value to us socially and culturally), their mode of practice must be understood and indeed practiced.[16]

In the case of international biennales, which encompass artworks from diverse cultures and conceptual foundations, keeping one foot firmly grounded in the here and now while also leading stakeholders (artists, participants, and viewers) along alternative routes is an exacting task. This is the current challenge for curators of biennales attuned to the issues of the day, which as a requirement of their implicitly transient directorial role they need to be.

Second, there is the carbon footprint of the exhibition itself to consider. If they have an environmental focus, the more ambitiously scaled exhibitions such as biennales risk being perceived as hypocritical unless a genuine and transparent attempt is made to reform traditional, resource-intensive exhibition staging. As T.J. Demos observes:

> Exhibitions dedicated to sustainability are fundamentally contradictory; for even as they seek to address climate change and work towards creative solutions – although certainly not all projects are equally

politically or pedagogically inclined – they contribute to the very problem of global warming by virtue of their own carbon footprint, the results of transporting artworks, maintaining the exhibition space's climate control and printing catalogues.[17]

Indeed, biennales are traditionally conceived and consumed as mega art exhibitions featuring major artworks by well-known artists, put together on huge budgets and leaving obnoxiously oversized carbon footprints. However, as the examples in this book reveal, curatorial practice in biennales is undergoing a major reformation of approach and methodology, one that is underpinned by more humility and less hubris. A new imperative on the part of artists and curators to reinvest art and exhibitions with cultural relevance has arisen in tandem with rapidly evolving social transformations currently in play – from young people across the world rising up against political inaction on climate change, to underemployment and depopulation of agricultural regions, and discontent with growing inequality. Slowly but surely, the elitism and arrogance that characterised aspects of biennale culture is being eroded in favour of a shared commitment to change.

In the face of crises, if curators are hoping to make positive change, they need to be optimistic. We can take heart from the fact that at the height of the COVID-19 pandemic there was extensive, ebullient coverage on social media video channels of animals coming in from the wild to repossess city spaces taken over by urban expansion. Having sent humans into lockdown to have a good hard think about their bad treatment of the planet, nature reasserted its preeminent position in the planet's ecology. We were also buoyed by Earth's response to widespread industrial stoppages and travel bans: momentarily, air and water quality improved significantly and carbon emissions plummeted. The enforced changes in human activity had an immediate and positive impact on the natural environment, demonstrating the capacity for humans to change their behaviours and for the planet to quickly begin to repair. This sense of optimism captured the mood for environmental change just prior to the pandemic: investors had begun cooling on fossil fuels, Greta Thunberg faced off Donald Trump at the World Economic Forum, young people embraced the School Strike for Climate movement, and local authorities declared climate emergencies in cities across the world.

Artists and curators themselves cannot change the world, but they do have the capacity to effect change. Maria Lind's concept of "the curatorial" as "a viral presence that strives to create friction and push new ideas" is usefully applied to the biennale model.[18] While acknowledging the limitations of curatorial projects to alter the direction of a society seemingly bent on self-destruction, *Curating in a Time of Ecological Crisis* builds on the recent momentum of environmental awareness by investigating how large-scale exhibitions of contemporary international art can be reimagined to not simply portray or despair over the many environmental challenges faced in the 21st century, but themselves generate new, more sustainable relations with the natural world.

Beyond the museum exhibitions discussed in Chapter 1, biennales are the subject of the book, specifically those with the financial resources and organisational commitment to position themselves as leaders. Historically, museums and gallery exhibitions have been society's key vehicle of engagement with the visual arts. As Patel et al. suggest, "it is perhaps the biennale exhibition that is the 'medium' through which new forms of art and artistic practice are introduced".[19] This is not a new proposition: biennales have for many years been acknowledged as having the incentive and capacity to embrace contemporary art at the more cutting edge of practice. Charles Green and Anthony Gardner's book *Biennials, Triennials and documenta* convincingly canvassed the increasing power of biennales to define contemporary art, noting that many visitors "encounter contemporary art solely within their frame".[20]

What is the role of the curator in this age in which international contemporary art is consumed primarily through the prism of biennales? No longer purely gatekeepers or arbiters of taste, today's curators of these most high-profile art events are responding in proactive, accessible, and engaging ways to the issues that preoccupy us, in particular those related to climate change. The book is divided into three chapters which collectively cover a number of standalone exhibitions (since the year 2000, Chapter 1) and recent biennales (Chapters 2 and 3). The case studies in the first chapter are drawn from major public galleries and art museums, these being the institutions with the resources to invest in ambitious curatorial projects and with the public profile to disseminate knowledge through exhibitions, and thereby impact audiences' understanding of how humankind can more effectively address climate change. Conversely, the biennales discussed in the ensuing chapters have been selected based not on the scale or notoriety of the exhibitions but on those biennales deploying new curatorial methodologies in the face of ecological crisis. For this reason, some of the smaller biennales without the resources to embrace curatorial experimentation, as well as major events which despite having generous budgets pursue a more conservative curatorial approach, are excluded.

In addition to a recent case study from Berlin that embraced a radically new exhibition model in response to ecological crises, the first chapter overviews noteworthy (non-biennale) environmental exhibitions staged in the United States in the late 1960s, as land art was emerging as a new genre, and in museums and public galleries in the United Kingdom and Australia in the early 2000s, just as those countries were starting to lead the global debate on the long-term and economic impacts of climate change. They have been selected for their scope, scale, and, most importantly, curatorial characteristics that define them as precursors of the new wave of biennales discussed in subsequent chapters.

The second chapter explores the concept of biennales as ecosystems: discrete exhibitions contained within mostly traditional exhibition spaces, comprising art projects often tightly bound – through participation and/or production – to the local communities in which the biennales are staged. The final chapter makes a case for the capacity of biennales to advance social empowerment and environmental sustainability in the communities of artists, participants, and consumers with which they partner. It demonstrates how new biennale paradigms can achieve lasting legacies.

While our political leaders continue to dither on addressing the ecological crisis, artists and curators are creating generative projects and exhibitions offering sustainable alternatives to how we might live. They bring a spirit of optimism in the wake of a pandemic that will forever alter our understanding of and interactions with each other, and with the threatened natural environments upon which we depend.

## Notes

1 Lecture attended by the author, School of Art & Design, University of New South Wales, 9 October, 2007.
2 Author's interview with Carolyn Christov-Bakargiev, Venice, 9 May, 2019.
3 Bruce Altshuler, "Introduction", in *Biennials and Beyond – Exhibitions That Made Art History*, London, Phaidon Press, 2013, p. 14.
4 Gavin Wade and Dave Beech (eds.), *Curating in the 21st Century*, Walsall, University of Wolverhampton New Art Gallery, 2000.
5 Hou Hanru, *Not Only Possible, But Also Necessary: Optimism in the Age of Global War – 10th Istanbul Biennial,* Istanbul, Istanbul Foundation for Culture and Arts, 2007, p. 25.
6 Julieta Aranda and Chus Martinez (eds.), "Latai Taumoepeau and Taloi Havini: The Last Resort – A Conversation", *e-flux Journal*, no. 112, October, 2020, www.e-flux.com/journal/112/ (accessed 25 August 2021).
7 Claire Doherty, "Curating Wrong Places . . . Or Where Have All the Penguins Gone?" in Paul O'Neill (ed.), *Curating x 24*, Amsterdam, De Appel, 2007.
8 Altshuler, "Introduction", p. 22.
9 Tessa Solomon, "Citing Surge in Covid Cases, Istanbul Biennial Postpones 2021 Edition", *ARTnews*, 6 May, 2021, www.artnews.com/art-news/news/istanbul-biennial-2021-edition-postponed-covid-1234592052/ (accessed 7 May 2021).
10 Curating Cities – a database of eco public art, http://eco-publicart.org
11 Tim Flannery, forum attended by the author, UNSW Centre for Ideas, Sydney, 19 August, 2020.
12 Chris McAuliffe, "Explainer: What is a Biennale?" *The Conversation*, 30 May, 2014, https://theconversation.com/explainer-what-is-a-biennale-26516 (accessed 30 January 2021).

13 Altshuler, "Introduction", p. 21.
14 Over the last decade, for example, the Venice Biennale's Arsenale collection of exhibition sites has progressively been cleaned up, the romantic lure of the old rope-making and ship-building facilities being of less interest than the art on display. In a surprising move, the Biennale of Sydney announced in 2021 that it would no longer be using as a venue the former ship-building precinct of Cockatoo Island. First identified and used as a Biennale site in 2008 by Carolyn Christov-Bakargiev, the island itself and the boat trip to reach it have been hugely popular with Biennale audiences.
15 Michael Baxandall, *Painting and Experience in Fifteenth-Century Italy*, Oxford, Oxford University Press, 1972, p. 41.
16 Shwetal A. Patel, Sunil Manghani and Robert E. D'Souza, *How to Biennale! (The Manual)*. A draft publication which accompanied a symposium at the Tate Exchange space in 2018 led by the Winchester School of Art. Ronald Kolb and Shwetal A. Patel (eds), "Draft: Global Biennial Survey 2018", *OnCurating*, issue 39, p. 11.
17 T.J. Demos, "The Politics of Sustainability: Art and Ecology", in Francesco Manacorda (ed.), *Radical Nature: Art and Architecture for a Changing Planet, 1969–2009*, Köln, Walther König, 2009, pp. 16–30.
18 Maria Lind, "Active Cultures: Maria Lind on The Curatorial", *Artforum*, October, 2009, p. 103.
19 Patel et al., *How to Biennale!* pp. 3–4.
20 Charles Green and Anthony Gardner, *Biennials, Triennials and Documenta: The Exhibitions That Created Contemporary Art*, Chichester, Wiley Blackwell, 2016, p. 3.

## Bibliography

Altshuler, Bruce, "Introduction", In *Biennials and Beyond – Exhibitions that Made Art History*, London, Phaidon Press, 2013.
Aranda, Julieta and Chus Martinez (eds.), "Latai Taumoepeau and Taloi Havini: The Last Resort – A Conversation", *e-flux Journal*, no. 112, October, 2020. www.e-flux.com/journal/112/
Baxandall, Michael, *Painting and Experience in Fifteenth-Century Italy*, Oxford, Oxford University Press, 1972.
Curating Cities – a database of eco public art. http://eco-publicart.org
Demos, T.J., "The Politics of Sustainability: Art and Ecology", In Francesco Manacorda (ed.), *Radical Nature: Art and Architecture for a Changing Planet, 1969–2009*, Köln, Walther König, 2009, pp. 16–30.
Doherty, Claire, "Curating Wrong Places . . . Or Where Have All the Penguins Gone?" In Paul O'Neill (ed.), *Curating x 24*, Amsterdam, De Appel, 2007.
Fenner, Felicity, interview with Carolyn Christov-Bakargiev, Venice, 9 May, 2019.
Flannery, Tim, UNSW Centre for Ideas, forum attended by the author, Sydney, 19 August, 2020.
Green, Charles and Anthony Gardner, *Biennials, Triennials and Documenta: The Exhibitions That Created Contemporary Art*, Chichester, Wiley Blackwell, 2016.
Hou, Hanru, *Not Only Possible, But Also Necessary: Optimism in the Age of Global War – 10th Istanbul Biennial*, Istanbul, Istanbul Foundation for Culture and Arts, 2007.

Lind, Maria, "Active Cultures: Maria Lind on the Curatorial", *Artforum*, October, 2009, p. 103.

McAuliffe, Chris, "Explainer: What is a Biennale?" *The Conversation*, 30 May, 2014. https://theconversation.com/explainer-what-is-a-biennale-26516

Patel, Shwetal A., Sunil Manghani and Robert E. D'Souza, *How to Biennale! (The Manual)*, Tate Exchange and Winchester School of Art, 2018.

Ronald Kolb and Shwetal A. Patel (eds), "Draft: Global Biennial Survey 2018", *OnCurating Issue* 39, pp. 9–14.

Solomon, Tessa, "Citing Surge in Covid Cases, Istanbul Biennial Postpones 2021 Edition", *ARTnews*, 6 May, 2021. www.artnews.com/art-news/news/istanbul-biennial-2021-edition-postponed-covid-1234592052/

Wade, Gavin and Dave Beech (eds.), *Curating in the 21st Century*, Walsall, University of Wolverhampton New Art Gallery, 2000.

# 1 Exhibiting Nature through the Decades

## From *Earthworks* (1968) to *Down to Earth* (2020)

The single largest challenge facing humans today is climate change. This chapter discusses major exhibitions responding to increasing global concern over the demise of our natural ecosystems, with a focus on those that began to appear with remarkable regularity in the early 2000s. Featuring art projects that bring together environmental activism and scientific knowledge, exhibitions staged in major museums and public galleries are well resourced to make speculative, cautionary, and occasionally optimistic predictions about the fate of the natural world and future viability of species, including Homo sapiens.

This first section overviews early curatorial forays into eco art, which in the 1960s largely existed under the banner of land art. It centres on two curated exhibitions in the United States as land art first came to the fore. The second section of the chapter discusses a handful of significant environmental exhibitions in the UK and Australia, both First World countries beginning in the early 2000s to assess the reality of climate change. Specifically, these were the first two countries in the world to commission detailed reports into the economic impacts of climate change, both of which were met with enormous publicity, controversy, and alarm. The resulting intensification of public outrage was the catalyst for a raft of environmental exhibitions in each country.[1] The final non-biennale curated exhibition considered here was staged in Berlin in 2020. *Down to Earth* is notable for its cavalier rejection of accepted standards of exhibition presentation in public art galleries and museums.

As narrators of our times, it is the role of artists and the curators of their work to be attuned to the issues of the day and, if public exhibitions of art are to engage broad audiences, to address them in ways that are well informed, thought-provoking, and perhaps even inspiring. While exhibitions are not traditionally perceived as conduits for the dissemination of ecological research, in the face of current crises they can and are being

DOI: 10.4324/9781003130574-2

deployed as fora for interpretation and knowledge transfer. How can this be done without depressing audiences and discouraging them from seeking the perspectives of artists in uncertain times? Many people still look to art – even art practice and exhibitions underpinned by a desire to raise awareness about environmental issues – to offer an apolitical reprieve from scientific data that is inevitably filled with dire predictions about the future of our planet. Those viewers are looking for glimmers of light, searching for hope in artists' commentaries and proposals, not despair.

If exhibitions are to be seriously engaged with, the exhibition curator must be cognisant of balancing naïve or overly cheerful assertions about the power of art to effect change with ecological realities: certainly artists as creative and lateral thinkers have proven themselves capable of proposing environmentally conscious projects that may be adopted by audiences and in turn may lead to behaviour change, or at least raise awareness around ecologically damaging lifestyle choices. Yet curators can only do so much to persuade audiences of the capacity of art to forestall the worst effects of climate change. While it is not the role of art to greenwash issues of ecological urgency, if art and exhibitions are to rise above the status of comforting distractions from the grim reality of an impending environmental catastrophe, they need to put their ideologies into practice. Returning to the original definition of the curator as one who cares, the current, sweeping transformations in society relating to the environmental movement, including the growing acceptance of green energies and respect for First Nations' knowledges around environmental stewardship, offer a timely opportunity for curatorial practice to redefine itself as an agent of change.

Obvious but important to remember is that artists are mostly not scientists and art exhibitions are not analysed in science journals. Rather, they are discussed, often quite subjectively, in the culture and entertainment pages of the mainstream media. In order to respect the conceptual intentions of the artist while not disengaging this core audience of cultural consumers, in weaving together artworks for display the curator must navigate a path underpinned by thematic rigour between visual captivation and subtle didacticism.

Since the first Echigo-Tsumari Art Triennale in Japan in 2000, a new generation of "biennales" (biennials and triennials) has initiated a diversity of curatorial models that embrace the growing environmental awareness among artists and society more broadly. In the late 20th century, many influential standalone art projects grew out of the land art movement, initiated by mostly independent and politically motivated artist practitioners. Four decades ago, for example, the now iconic projects in Manhattan by Agnes Denes and Alan Sonfist, and in Kassel by Joseph Beuys, emboldened artists to advance environmental issues through direct action.[2] With few exceptions, it was not until some decades later, however, as environmental concerns became mainstream social and political issues, that major public institutions began staging exhibitions in response to growing public interest, employing curatorial methodologies to convey information and open new dialogues around the ecological crisis.

## Pioneering Curators of Environmental Art: The United States in the Late 1960s

Prior to the first Echigo-Tsumari Art Triennale in the year 2000, which heralded the 21st-century swing towards biennale-led programmes focused on sustainability, the vast majority of eco art projects were initiated by artists, usually a sole artist, and staged outside traditional biennale or gallery and museum frameworks. Very few environmentally themed projects were taken up by curators: the forced resignation of curator Sam Wagstaff in 1971 following the unilateral hostile response to Michael Heizer's land art project in Detroit validated concerns that controversial environmental statements had no place in art institutions.[3]

Yet some of the few exhibitions led by curators prior to Wagstaff's dismissal are noteworthy for their role as precursors to the international biennales that have since foregrounded ecological crises. Riding the wave of social and political changes that culminated in the mass protests of 1968, a small cohort of pioneering curators advanced the acceptance of environmental art by curating it into exhibitions more broadly interested in the then emerging genre of conceptual art, which often included found materials from the natural world. Adopting the concept of the gallery as a laboratory for research and experimentation, the US exhibitions can in retrospect be recognised as important testing grounds for new models of curatorial practice.

These curatorial experiments date back to when the concept of global warming was first being mooted by scientists and few conduits existed for dissemination of knowledge from the scientific community to the general public. One key catalyst was the publication of American biologist and conservationist Rachel Carson's books on the natural environment, in particular *Silent Spring* (1962), which first threw light on the danger to natural ecosystems of using chemicals in agriculture. An accomplished scientist, Carson revealed to the world the toxic impact of the widely used pesticide DDT, her publication attracting fierce opposition from chemical companies yet eventually leading to the establishment of the US Government's Environmental Protection Agency (EPA) and triggering more broadly the environmental movement.

While the potential for human-produced carbon dioxide ($CO_2$) to have a detrimental effect on the climate was noted by scientists back in the late

19th century, scientific data to corroborate that possibility was not collected until the 1950s, when $CO_2$ emissions readings established the reality of global warming. Yet even into the 1960s climate change was not agreed upon among scientists and was met with scepticism, if registered at all, by the wider community. It was not until the mid-1970s that the term "global warming" entered the public domain and not until 1988 that the Intergovernmental Panel on Climate Change (IPCC) was established.[4] With its beginnings in the late 1960s, land art was, as is often the case with art, representing if not leading the tide of change in attitudes towards the environment. Curatorial practice, also not unusually, was running to keep up with trailblazing artists: only a handful of curators had the vision and means to support artists whose work responded to the burgeoning environmental movement, staging small but seminal exhibitions such as *Earthworks* (1968) and *Earth Art* (1969). With these exhibitions, curators provided venues, financial support, and new audiences, amplifying and disseminating the ideas of those artists who were becoming increasingly concerned for the future of planet Earth.

On the 60th anniversary of the publication of *Silent Spring*, it is timely to remember that it was Carson's status as an outsider and her ability to communicate her findings in an accessible and engaging way through her books (as artists do using visual media) that were essential to her success in cutting through the obstacles thrown in her path by the largely anti-environmental scientific community. In her introduction to the 40th anniversary edition of *Silent Spring*, Carson's biographer stressed the role of her relative independent status in reaching broad audiences.

> Carson was an outsider who had never been part of the scientific establishment, first because she was a woman but also because her chosen field, biology, was held in low esteem in the nuclear age. Her career path was non-traditional; she had no academic affiliation, no institutional voice. She deliberately wrote for the public rather than for a narrow scientific audience. For anyone else, such independence would have been an enormous detriment. But by the time *Silent Spring* was published, Carson's outsider status had become a distinct advantage.[5]

Artists, like writers such as Carson, have the opportunity to be influential thought leaders, operating as they do outside the dominant structures of capitalism that prop up non-sustainable industries and self-interested consumers. Since the 1960s, many artists have been positioning environmental issues at the core of their practice, a genre already well established as integral to the history of art in the second half of the 20th century. With few exceptions, however, curators were much slower than individual artists or artist collectives to make environmental matters the focus of their projects. The role of the curator in public art museums and galleries has traditionally been one of organising exhibitions of existing artworks either borrowed or drawn from the organisation's own collection. Until recent decades, when innovative and collaborative curatorial approaches began to be adopted by international biennales, art in museum and public gallery exhibitions was rarely commissioned specifically for the exhibition.

The curatorial role in many of the significant early environmental exhibitions was recorded in a 2012 largely archival exhibition curated in the United States that set out to investigate "the art *and* curatorial activities of the 1960s and 1970s to glean the conditions that contributed to the favourable promotion of land art as a viable new art category".[6] *Ends of the Earth: Land Art to 1974* was curated by Philipp Kaiser and Miwon Kwon and presented at the Museum of Contemporary Art in Los Angeles (2012) and the Haus der Kunst in Munich (2013). The exhibition of work by more than 100 artists from the United States, Europe, Iceland, Israel, and Japan was the most comprehensive survey to date of land art. It comprised photographic prints and slides, and films and texts recording temporary and performative works. There was also a selection of original hand-drawn works and a sprinkling of installations made from organic materials by artists such as Barry Flanagan, Hans Haacke, and Günther Uecker. The key historical exhibitions discussed here were documented in detail both curatorially within the exhibition and in the definitive publication, a valuable resource on early environmental art.[7]

One of the first public museum exhibitions of environmental art was the 1969 *Earth Art* exhibition at the Andrew Dickson White Museum of Art at Cornell University in Ithaca, New York. The exhibition followed one the previous year organised by commercial gallery dealer and major art patron Virginia Dwan, *Earthworks*, which was staged entirely indoors yet each of the works featured earth elements, mostly soil. It was the catalyst for subsequent ambitious, large-scale constructions in the land by artists such as Heizer, Walter de Maria, and Robert Smithson. Dwan was conscious at the time that art was moving out of the white cube of the gallery and that environmental art was only truly meaningful when sited in the natural environment. Over four decades later, writing for the catalogue of the *Ends of the Earth* exhibition, in explaining the absence of some leading land art artists' work from that exhibition, she remained adamant that "the photograph is not the work".[8] Dwan's support for the first generation of American environmental artists is acknowledged as playing a key role in launching the land art movement.

At the time, curator Seth Siegelaub also showcased land art as part of a curatorial programme with a primary purpose of promoting the new, contemporary movement of conceptual art. The programme included installation-based projects on two college campuses in 1968 that also echoed the concurrent *Earthworks* exhibition, with artists working site-specifically in natural environments.⁹ For *Earth Art* the following year, curator Willoughby Sharp took the next step in advancing a new genre of environmental art by inviting artists to work both inside the museum and outdoors around the campus, using found materials from the natural environment. Key artists included Heizer, Dennis Oppenheim and Smithson, who the following year created the seminal *Spiral Jetty* sculptural intervention that became an emblem of "land art", a term that only came into being around 1969.¹⁰ The curatorial decision to extend the exhibition outdoors into the landscape effectively dissolved physical and symbolic barriers between culture and nature, drawing attention to the potential for art to become part of nature rather than simply reflect on it from the comfort of a gallery interior, or impose upon the land in ways that are aesthetically or environmentally burdensome. This approach echoes the simultaneous, albeit still evolving acknowledgement that human life is inextricably bound to the natural world.

What is interesting about these few exhibitions of the late 1960s, one presented by a commercial gallery dealer who was also a major art patron and the others in the context of university art programmes, is that all were initiated from within the art industry. Although the concepts and intentions of the invited artists' various practices were underpinned by social and political imperatives to raise awareness in the general population of humanity's inherent relationship with nature, these artworks do not and could not have existed without financial and curatorial support from the art world, even though it was a world to which land art was very new and not yet fully accepted. Artists need the platform of curated exhibitions for their voices to be heard. Today, international biennales are the principal stages for disseminating the ideas of contemporary artists.

Harald Szeemann's influential exhibition of anti-object, found-material conceptual art in 1969 cemented the status of art as a new genre of practice that aligned with contemporary art more broadly. *Live in Your Head. When Attitudes Become Form: Works – Concepts – Processes – Situations – Information* was not an exhibition of environmental or land art, but it brought into its fold leading proponents of the movement such as Heizer, Joseph Beuys, Richard Long, and Smithson. Staged at the Kunsthalle Bern in Switzerland and subsequently at the Institute of Contemporary Arts in London, the exhibition has in the fullness of time been recognised as a gamechanger in curatorial practice, having rejected the idea of art as either object or commodity. By including work by key practitioners of the burgeoning group of land artists into a museum exhibition initiated by a trendsetting curator of contemporary art, their practice was given legitimacy and its status elevated, if not to the mainstream at least onto the art world's radar.

Early exhibitions of land art marked a shift in curatorial approaches to the presentation of art from one that was essentially authorial to one of collaboration. As Willoughy Sharp, curator of *Earth Art*, explained in an interview some years later, unprecedented trust was placed in the artists by the curator:

> The way I curated the show was: I decided whom I wanted: I asked them if they would be in the show, and what they wanted to do, and most of them had a fairly vague idea of what they wanted to do – just coming and going to Ithaca and looking over the land and then executing a work. Down the line they would specify what they needed – some plants, some earth, some wood, and whatever it was they need to build their piece. . . . I never questioned these artists about their work and I trusted them to all to deliver it.[11]

In a shift from traditional curatorial practice, Sharp did not identify and select particular artworks for the exhibition. Instead, he invited artists with an essentially environmentally focused practice to create something for the exhibition. This move away from a process of selecting and arranging to instead identifying key artists and placing trust in them to deliver a responsive, socially relevant project, began simultaneously with the emergence of land art. It has been noted elsewhere that "this new manner of assembling exhibitions had much to do with the nature of the art being shown, with processed-based works . . . having to be produced on site".[12] Later, this level of faith in artists became a hallmark of biennales. In the context of the biennales discussed in the following chapters, it becomes apparent that the "curatorial thinking" required for working with land art in the 1960s foregrounded the exhibition-making methodologies underpinning the recent raft of ecologically aware biennales.

As these few early exhibitions additionally reveal, curators more interested in conceptual art were often also promoting the work of environmental art under the same banner. The dematerialised, non-commercial, and politically engaged aspect of land art aligned with the shift by a new generation of conceptual artists away from traditional art world tropes of making and presenting art objects, and a new generation of collaborating curators willing to trust them.

Beyond the gallery walls, it was Heizer's *Dragged Mass Displacement* of 1971 that first made an impact, not in nature or within the white cube of an art institution, but in the public domain of the city centre. A controversial action that was ultimately unresolved, the work involved a colossal granite block being dragged by tractors across the grass outside the Detroit Institute of Arts. The block was intended to dig into and become embedded in the ground but failed to do so. Instead, it destroyed a manicured lawn, leaving onlookers baffled and civic authorities furious. In hauling a granite block across the lawn, Heizer mimicked an act of violence to make a point about humankind's destruction of nature. But this is where the project ended: the earth below was revealed by ripping up the grass, yet the life-giving properties of the soil were not investigated or used to demonstrate more sustainable usages of the land. Unlike Olafur Eliasson's icebergs dragged from the Arctic into European cities almost 50 years later, Heizer's project was seen not as an environmentally enlightened gesture but as a brutal act of destruction, with the public backlash and disapproval from the Institute's board of trustees soon forcing the resignation of the project's curator.[13]

Though it may not have met with its intended reception at the time – and its political intent was less overt than Eliasson's – Heizer's action illustrated the role of artists in creating visual impact in unexpected sites to highlight issues that may not otherwise attract public debate. In this way, the work can be seen as an important precursor to art projects that not only mimic human exploitation of natural environments but also propose alternative, more ecologically sustainable interactions with nature. Over three decades later, for example, artist Fritz Haeg began tearing up the front gardens of private houses, this time in willing collaboration with the stakeholders, the homes' owners. Rather than destroying the lawn solely for the purpose of making a point, in his *Edible Estates* project (2005–2014) Haeg worked with the residents to replace the lawns with functional kitchen gardens that offer positive environmental, community, economic as well as physical and mental health benefits.[14] These two projects, undertaken two generations apart, demonstrate that it is often artists who have the imagination and skill set to conceive and develop projects that draw attention in the public domain to natural ecosystems and, at least in the case of the latter project, have the capacity to effect change.

## A Cautionary Tale: Beuys' *7000 Oaks* and the 1984 Biennale of Sydney

Historically, biennales have struggled to support environmental projects intended to have lasting impact. The most famous exception is Joseph Beuys' *7000 Oaks: City Forestation Instead of City Administration* (*7000 Eichen: Stadtverwaldung statt Stadverwaltung*). It was created for documenta in 1982, the first permanent environmental art project initiated under the auspices of a recurrent temporary exhibition, in this case not a biennial but Germany's quinquennial event and the world's leading platform for contemporary art.

Less widely known is that two years later, *7000 Oaks* was curated into the 1984 Biennale of Sydney. Lacking support from either the commissioning art institution or civic authorities, however, the work was all but ignored, mostly forgotten over the ensuing decades and almost removed to make way for building works in the early 2020s.

Forty years after its launch in Kassel, *7000 Oaks* is widely recognised as one of the world's most influential environmental art projects, not least for its ongoing legacy which saw 7,000 trees planted in the city of Kassel over five years.[15] The project has become a beacon for environmental artists internationally. Kassel had been badly bombed in World War Two. *7000 Oaks* fostered a caring approach to nature and the environment by greening the rebuilt areas of the city. The artist's instructions were for each oak tree to be paired with a columnar basalt stone of around four feet high, both the oak and the stone symbolising resilience over time, the stone also serving to identify each tree as part of the *7000 Oaks* project. Civic authorities were initially concerned that the trees might obstruct public rights of way and inhibit future urban planning, as well as undermine government control over urban space.[16] Today, the project is acknowledged worldwide and by the city of Kassel for its ecological significance and is well maintained by the city with some trees being replaced with new or alternative specimens where the originals failed to flourish.

It was always Beuys' intention to extend the project globally, with culturally significant tree species being selected for each site based on the local historical and environmental context. Beuys brought the project first to Australia with a single tree and accompanying basalt stone column instated on the lawn in front of the Art Gallery of New South Wales (AGNSW) in central Sydney in 1984. A few years later in 1988, the Dia Art Foundation in New York installed five basalt stones paired with five trees at 548 West 22nd Street, adding 25 trees and stones on West 22nd Street in 1996, as well as seven stones to pre-existing trees. In 1998, a single tree and basalt stone column were installed in Leeds, UK, next to the Leeds Art Gallery and the Henry Moore Institute. In 2021, another pair of trees was added in New York as part of the major Dia Chelsea renovation. In Sydney a fig tree was chosen; in New York a variety of street tree species have been installed; and in Leeds the original oak species was selected.[17]

Australia's small but valued version of *7000 Oaks*, as the first international iteration comprising a solo tree that has survived against the odds, has a beleaguered history worth recounting as a warning about the fragility of long-term environmental legacy art projects initiated within the short-term framework of exhibitions such as biennales.

The tree is one of a handful that frames the classical façade of the late 19th-century AGNSW. They are all Moreton Bay figs, enormous banyan trees native to the south-eastern seaboard of the continent with a lifespan of more than 100 years. Some of the trees in the vicinity of the gallery were planted in the mid-1800s, 50 years before construction of the gallery even began. The smallest of the Moreton Bay figs flanking the gallery is the only iteration in the Southern Hemisphere of Beuys' environmental art project: *7000 Oaks* is one of his last major works and also the most far-reaching. It is an art-led ecological intervention and occupation of public space intended to raise awareness about the environment by offering first-hand experience of nature and its life cycles within an urban context.

Leon Paroissien, artistic director of the 1984 Biennale of Sydney, commissioned Sydney's tree on behalf of the Biennale of Sydney. The Biennale appointed René Block as commissioner for Germany that year to advise on content and recommend particular artists and works. Paroissien had seen the beginnings of *7000 Oaks* in Kassel and enthusiastically supported Block's suggestion that Sydney be the first city to host an international iteration of the project.[18] The work aligned perfectly with the thematic premise of his exhibition *Private Symbol: Social Metaphor*, which championed not primarily political works but art concerned with social issues of which artists had personal insight or experience. A pioneer of the environmental movement, Beuys was a founding member of the German Green Party, advocating for the greening of cities and recycling of consumable products in the 1970s, well before such initiatives became civic and mainstream political issues.[19]

In 2015, the AGNSW hired Japanese architectural firm SANAA, led by Kazuyo Sejima and Ryue Nishizawa working in association with Architectus in Sydney, to design a new extension. In late 2018, following extensive consultation, including with the City of Sydney and curators keen to have the Beuys work saved, a revised design was approved: rather than removing the tree as originally proposed, the new design retains and recognises Beuys' tree, celebrating its significance as an iconic project of the environmental art movement.

The third oldest in the world after Venice (1895) and São Paulo (1951), Sydney's was Australia's first (1973) and remains the country's leading international biennale.[20] From the beginning, the Biennale of Sydney adopted a proactive policy to include temporary and site-specific environmental art in public spaces, with the early biennales setting a precedent for inviting international environmental artists to create works for Australia.[21] The 1976 Biennale of Sydney curator Tom McCullough commissioned a fog sculpture by Japanese artist Fujiko Nakaya, originally shown in the parklands opposite the gallery and subsequently acquired for permanent installation at the National Gallery of Australia in Canberra.[22] As part of the 1979 Biennale, curated by British-born Nick Waterlow, English land artist Hamish Fulton undertook and documented a walk in Tasmania, and Scottish artist Mark Boyle (later exhibiting as a member of the Boyle Family), having represented Great Britain at the previous year's Venice Biennale, travelled to Central Australia to create a new work for the Biennale based on the desert landscape.[23]

In Kassel, Beuys chose oak trees because of their historic significance in Europe. "It has always been a form of sculpture, a symbol for this planet ever since the Druids, who are called after the oak. Druid means oak. They used their oaks to define their holy places."[24] For Sydney, Beuys decided upon the specific species of tree in consultation with local advisers. The artist did have first-hand experience of the geography, having visited a couple of years earlier for the installation of his work *Stripes from the House of the Shaman* (1964–1972) at the National Gallery of Australia. Beuys and the project team sought a tree with a similar historic link to place and selected the *Ficus macrophyilla*. Colloquially known as the Moreton Bay fig, it is as large and slow-growing as a European oak.

Geographer Matthew Gandy claims that the original *7000 Oaks* project "cannot be satisfactorily interpreted without considering the way in which nature aesthetics has been repeatedly combined with nationalist sentiment in European environmental discourse".[25] In the cultural context of early 1980s Australia when *7000 Oaks* was proposed for Sydney, however, nature aesthetics in art was more aligned with international art trends than nationalist sentiment. (Despite inclusion in earlier Sydney biennales, it was not until the 1990s that the art of Aboriginal artists, which is largely informed by the natural world, began to be included more broadly in exhibitions of Australian contemporary art.) While the oak tree in Europe may for some have nationalist connotations, the same is not true of the Moreton Bay fig tree, nor of Beuys' intentions in using it in Sydney. While there is no record of who proposed the Moreton Bay fig to Beuys, we do know that the artist dismissed the use of an imported oak tree as lacking relevance to Sydney and that the decision to substitute it with the local native species was one unanimously agreed upon by all parties and facilitated by the Royal Botanic Garden, AGNSW's next-door neighbour.[26] As well as being synonymous with the enduring landscape of Sydney and having featured in Australian painting for generations, the distinctive tree has been culturally significant to the First Nations people of the coastal lands around Sydney for over 60,000 years. The Gadigal of the Eora Nation traditionally made fishing nets from the tree fibres.[27] Given its ubiquity around Sydney and with a history enmeshed in both Aboriginal and post-settlement cultural tradition, the Moreton Bay fig was, in Paroissien's words, the "obvious choice".[28]

By 1984 the artist was too ill to travel to Sydney, so René Block planted the tree on Beuys' behalf during that year's Biennale. The tree was sited to address the gallery's portico, presumably as a reference to the original

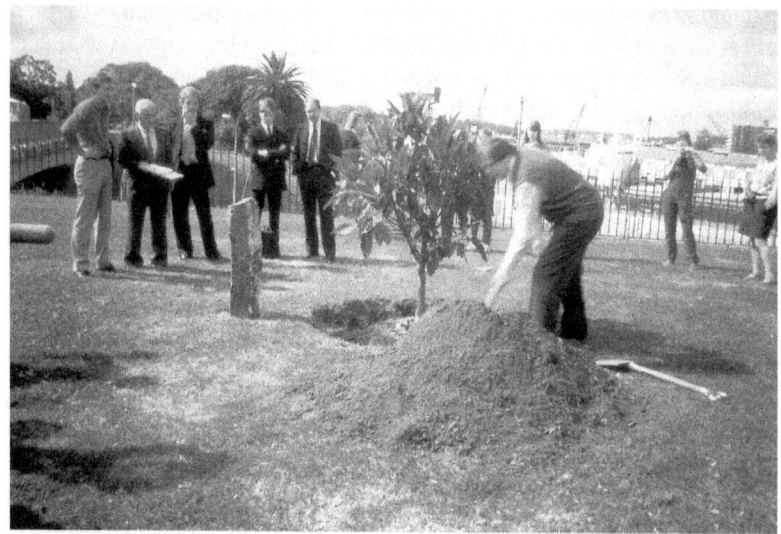

*Figure 1.1* René Block installing *7000 Oaks* on behalf of Joseph Beuys. 3rd Biennale of Sydney (1984). Observers in the background (left to right) are Leon Paroissien, Franco Belgiorno-Nettis, Edmund Capon, Timothy D'Offay and Anthony D'Offay.

Source: Courtesy Biennale of Sydney.

gathering of basalt stones in Kassel which had similarly been oriented to the classical portico of the Museum Fridericianum, and to provide a dialogue between nature and culture in relation to the nearby Henry Moore bronze *Reclining Figure: Angles*.[29] Block provided the accompanying basalt stone column (or "stele") and shipped it to Australia along with other works for the 1984 Biennale. It was installed adjacent to the tree, in the same way as the basalt stones are paired with Beuys' oak trees throughout Kassel. In 1988 – the exact date and circumstance remains shrouded in mystery – the stone was removed, its significance presumably unappreciated by the Royal Botanic Garden, the authority responsible for greenspace around the AGNSW. Block later tracked down the stone and found it languishing in a Botanic Garden storage unit along with other discarded civic stones and statues.[30] At the conclusion of the 1990 Biennale of Sydney that Block had curated, with the tree "de-Beuysed" by local authorities, Block returned the stone column to Berlin for safe-keeping, shipping it home with other artworks from the Biennale. Thanks to some research and detective work initiated in 2017 by Mami Kataoka, the basalt stone column is being reinstated and the original work relaunched as part of the gallery's Sydney Modern extension of 2022, exactly 40 years after Beuys created the work for documenta.

This sequence of events over many decades demonstrates the need for ongoing curatorial vigilance around legacy projects installed as part of a biennale, which all too easily fall victim to changes in civic and cultural priorities. As the history of Sydney's iteration of *7000 Oaks* demonstrates, ownership and ongoing responsibility for such projects must be meticulously articulated and agreed to from the outset if today's public artworks are to be protected from tomorrow's public foibles.

## Recent Museum Exhibitions

By the late 2000s, the possibility of an impending ecological crisis was amplified by government-commissioned reports into its potential impact. In the UK, the Stern Review (2006) was the first analysis by an economist of the impact of climate change not just on the planet but on the economy.[31] While there had been earlier reports flagging the economic decline in the face of climate change, the detailed analysis and predictions provided by Stern prompted immediate action by the UK government to curb carbon emissions and encourage other countries to do the same. In Australia, economist Ross Garnaut released a draft report in 2008 proposing an Emissions Trading Scheme, identifying Australia's natural environment and agriculture sector as being particularly at risk if global emissions were not significantly reduced. In 2010, the final Garnaut Review was criticised by economists who accused it of overstating the financial impact of global warming and by environmentalists for understating the level of commitment required to avoid a catastrophic ecological crisis.

Nicholas Bourriaud's 1999 publication on socially engaged art, *Relational Aesthetics*, influenced a raft of major (non-biennale) environmentally themed exhibitions that began to be curated within and beyond art museums and galleries.[32] They were propelled by the heightened social awareness of pressing environmental challenges and facilitated by rapidly eroding boundaries between the museum and the public domain. Extending curated exhibitions beyond the gallery walls, art institutions seized the opportunity to apply the principles of public engagement in projects that not only reflected on but also sought through educational and socially engaged practice to change perceptions of our relationship to the natural world.

One of the first major curated exhibitions was at the Barbican Centre in London, in 2009. A survey of environmentalist art from over the previous 40 years, *Radical Nature: Art and Architecture for a Changing Planet 1969–2009* brought together political and speculative proposals by mostly

European artists for reimagining our connection with and floundering control over nature. Curated by Francesco Manacorda, the core institutional exhibition included projects from Beuys and Smithson through to contemporaries Anya Gallaccio and Simon Starling. Writing for *Frieze*, Stephen Beasley concluded that *Radical Nature*

> could be mistaken for the research and development wing of some insane urban scientist with an extreme prejudice against nature [revealing that] since the late 1960s our attitude toward nature has been inspired or inflected by an increasing self-awareness that we're all directly or indirectly fucking it up.[33]

Expanding the exhibition beyond the museum in a desire to actively rather than passively engage audiences in the issues being explored by the exhibition and to also propose achievable solutions, the Barbican ambitiously commissioned a contemporary, local interpretation of Agnes Denes' *Wheatfield – A Confrontation* (Battery Park, Manhattan, 1982).[34] The curators sourced a patch of vacant land adjacent to a decommissioned railway line in Dalston, an area in the East End of London then undergoing gentrification and major development ahead of the 2012 London Olympic Games.

Designed by French architecture collective EXYST, *Dalston Mill* was just one of a few artworks in the *Radical Nature* exhibition to be sited in the public arena, though the only one some distance from the Barbican Centre and easily the most ambitious in scale and impactful in its legacy. It was curated in association with the Royal Society of Arts (RSA) Arts & Ecology programme, run by Michaela Crimmin, a British curator committed to advancing environmental sustainability through contemporary art projects. As Head of Arts at the RSA, Crimmin commissioned the first three sculptures of the Fourth Plinth project in Trafalgar Square and founded the Arts & Ecology Centre for the RSA and Arts Council England. Crimmin's commitment to ecological and public art was well known to Manacorda from when he studied under her on the Royal College of Art's Curating Contemporary Art Program in the early 2000s.

Manacorda described the site for the *Dalston Mill* project as one of "urban collision with the rural" and explained that "it was essential to the exhibition to get art outside and to get nature inside". Revealing a more political motivation, EXYST architect Nicholas Henninger stated from the outset that a key aim of the project was to impart knowledge about growing and preparing food that could then be applied and shared at home.[35] As such, the premise of the project was less performative than it was didactic, offering possibilities for urban regeneration through artist-led activity.

Though commissioned as part of a traditional art exhibition, this project was staged in public space primarily for the benefit of the local community. Working in close collaboration with Agnes Denes, Crimmin ensured that EXYST reimagined Denes' original *Wheatfield* for a new generation and very different plot of land that allowed only a 20-metre field, in contrast to the two acres in Manhattan 27 years earlier. The Dalston site was further distinguished from Battery Park by its relatively dense residential population. Crimmin and the architects also took the project a step further than Denes' purely agricultural imperative, building a temporary wind turbine that powered the flour mill that in turn ground the wheat harvested from the earth. They set up a commercial-grade oven, baked bread, and served it in a makeshift café. There was a temporary bar on the weekends, pedal-powered music and a programme of live events including performances by a local youth theatre, urban psychoanalysis workshops on Dalston run by artist-urbanist Laurent Petit, and baking and cake-decorating demonstrations.

Unlike the Manhattan site of *Wheatfield*, the project's historical precedent and inspiration, the popularity of the three-week-long *Dalston Mill* activity led to the plot of land on which it was staged being retained as a community garden. The local council was persuaded by the success of the initial project and retained the original team including EXYST lead architect Henninger to create a permanent garden for local residents and visitors to the area. While entry is free to all, its café, pizza oven, and bar ensure commercial viability.

The evolution of the temporary *Dalston Mill* to the permanent Dalston Eastern Curve Garden would likely not have been possible 50 years ago, when urban development was allowed to run rampant with little consideration for people's need to connect with natural environments. This shift in priorities and the increased agency of organisers such as curators and in this case architects to advocate for and achieve ecologically positive results for the land and the community who value it is concurrent with the evolution of environmental art into the mainstream. Artists who created single-entity environmental or land art projects in the past worked without the support of museums and their curatorial gatekeepers, which in turn limited their capacity to effect permanent change. The Dalston Eastern Curve Garden is a modest yet significant marker of a shift in urban planning that has occurred in recent years, which has seen art and curatorial projects not only propose but also achieve greater appreciation of and public access to greenery.

Another project that used urban agriculture as a catalyst for sustainable social change was the aforementioned Fritz Haeg's *Edible Estates*, a component of which was undertaken in London (2007). Like *Dalston Mill*, it too was part of a large public institutional exhibition, having been commissioned by Tate Modern for its *Global Cities* exhibition project. Haeg's mission to help individuals to grow their own food had commenced a couple of years before in the United States, the artist working with private individuals to transform traditional front lawns into vegetable gardens, but it was the imprimatur and high profile of Tate Modern that brought world attention to the project. In central London, the garden was established on a triangular lawn belonging to the Brookwood House Council Estate with the intention that everyone would be able to see, participate in, and reap the rewards of the project. In a high density, disadvantaged area of south London, the production of food became a public spectacle. In the years following, it invited not only resident participants but passers-by to reconsider their connection to the land and how they inhabit it. As residents and community members come and go, the garden is still thriving in the early 2020s.

These two legacy projects in London are rare: despite well-intentioned curatorial strategies to advance knowledge around and behaviour change towards the natural environment, it is generally beyond the scope of exhibitions organised by institutional museum curators to nurture long-term, permanent projects in the public domain. Other standalone exhibitions, nevertheless, have been relatively successful in drawing attention to impending and current ecological crises, though the receivers of this information are largely restricted to existing art audiences that habitually visit museum and public gallery exhibitions.

In the same year as the Barbican's *Radical Nature* exhibition, the Royal Academy of Arts (RA) staged *Earth: Art of a Changing World*. Like most museum-bound exhibitions, *Earth* aimed to illustrate, rather than propose solutions to what was then perceived as an encroaching ecological crisis. As the Editorial in the conservative *Spectator* asked at the time, "Could such an exhibition, held prominently in one of the global capitals of the world at the centre of the controversy, actually do much to extend this narrative?"[36] The answer is "no": despite its rollcall of prominent artists – including Mona Hatoum, Cornelia Parker, and Tomas Saraceno – this was a collection of pre-existing artworks that until being assembled together on the premise of responding to imminent environmental catastrophe had been created for and exhibited in very different contexts. Most obviously, Anthony Gormley's army of small terracotta figures, *Field*, which has since 1991 been re-created and exhibited in different parts of the world, served here (despite always being an impressive installation) to dilute the ecological focus of the exhibition.

Selecting existing artworks for a thematic exhibition was the abiding function of the traditional curator, who historically worked within the purview of museum collections. While contemporary curators of museum and public gallery exhibitions now have the capacity to proactively commission new works for specified curatorial projects, including for the public domain, most still tend to revert to selecting and presenting existing artworks within the gallery walls and creating, in the best case scenarios, a conversation or dialogue between those works that will hopefully also engage viewers.

*Earth: Art of a Changing World* exemplified this traditional approach, despite the forward-looking theme of the exhibition. Rather than proposing new understandings of and relationships with our natural ecosystems, "the exhibition reflected the impact of the climate change debate on the practice of a broad range of contemporary artists".[37] The terms used by organisers to describe the intentions and outcomes of the exhibition further confirmed its purpose as one of reflection, advancing the long-established role of the artist as a "communicator, reflector and interpreter of key issues of the day".[38]

The following year, Sydney's Museum of Contemporary Art (MCA) presented a similarly conceived exhibition, *In the Balance: Art for a Changing World*. The title is a hybrid appropriation from Al Gore's influential book of 1992 *Earth in the Balance: Ecology and the Human Spirit* (the basis of his better-known lecture series and film *An Inconvenient Truth*) and the RA exhibition that preceded the MCA's.

Disparate projects by around 30 mostly Australian artists and artist collectives were surveyed in a traditional gallery-based approach. A substantial portion of the exhibition was the presentation of multi-generational art addressing environmental activism in Tasmania since the 1960s. The impact on the land of industry was briefly considered, the principal contribution being David McKenzie and Susan Norrie's harrowing video installation documenting an ongoing, mining-led mudslide in Indonesia, made some years earlier for the 2007 Venice Biennale.[39] The other key theme was waterways, with a focus on Australia's precious yet severely compromised and politically contentious Murray–Darling River system. In this section of the exhibition, traditional First Nations' experience and knowledge about water care and sustainability were foregrounded in works on paper depicting cultural stories of the river and in traditionally woven fish and eel traps.

In revealing evidence of ecological destruction through images and, to a lesser extent, offering alternative, more sustainable solutions for inhabiting the world, *In the Balance* asked audiences "to think carefully about how we wish to envision our future" as citizens of the world rather than mere observers of it.[40] While 80 percent of the exhibition comprised gallery exhibits, a handful of projects were either commissioned by the MCA or initiated by individual artists including for outdoor spaces. While not necessarily conceived as projects that would themselves have a lifespan beyond the duration of the exhibition, they did create a legacy in terms of introducing individuals and communities to more environmentally sustainable approaches to sourcing and discarding food and consumer items. These

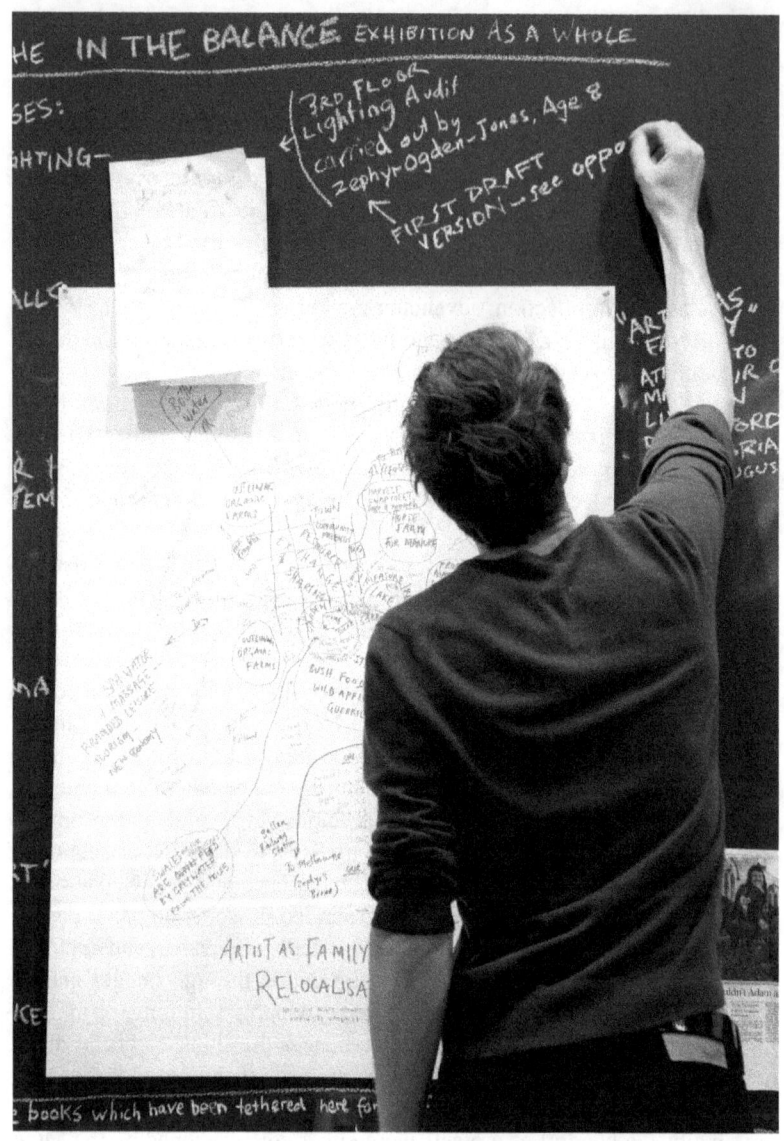

*Figure 1.2* Lucas Ihlein, *Environmental Audit*, 2010 (detail), *In the Balance: Art for a Changing World*, Museum of Contemporary Art Australia, 2010.

Photograph: Silversalt.

included artist-led walking tours of the city to discover and learn about native flora and fauna, a wild permaculture food garden in Surry Hills, and an installation by Dutch artist Jeanne van Heeswijk based on a community-based project about waste and landfill, originally commissioned by MCA senior curator Anne Loxley for the Museum's C3 West programme.[41]

Finally, the exhibition itself bravely adopted a self-reflexive tone, contracting one artist to monitor and issue a report card on its environmental footprint. As T.J. Demos argued in his catalogue essay for the Barbican's *Radical Nature* exhibition, when comprising art objects arranged in a traditional museum display, "eco art exhibitions are simply unviable from an environmental perspective".[42] Artist Lucas Ihlein responded the following year in his approach to *In the Balance*:

> If the MCA is going to put together an exhibition about the environment and climate change, I think the question that everybody will ask is this: how many resources were consumed in delivering the message?[43]

The audit consisted mainly of a blog and a series of printed diagrams detailing carbon emissions, exhibited in the MCA within the exhibition. At the close of the exhibition, Ihlein refrained from declaring whether, given its carbon footprint, the staging of *In the Balance* was justified from an environmental point of view. Ihlein was drafted again a decade later to champion a "plastic free" 2020 Biennale of Sydney.[44]

The MCA exhibition acknowledged the potential of art to foster behaviour change in the wider community. However, it stopped short of initiating projects that may have had positive impacts beyond its duration: such projects require long-term responsibility for care and maintenance, which is a major obstacle for the survival of legacy projects commissioned for museum and temporary exhibitions, as discussed earlier in relation to Beuys and the Biennale of Sydney.

Also preceding *In the Balance* was *HEAT: Art and Climate Change* at Australia's Royal Melbourne Institute of Technology (RMIT) gallery in 2008. The exhibition's curatorial proposition was that the public messaging around climate change by scientists and the media is changing how humans think about themselves in relation to the natural world. It featured work by 19 artists and artist collectives derived mostly from Australia, with a sprinkling of contributions from the northern hemisphere including by David Buckland and Max Eastley of Cape Farewell in the UK, who were subsequently involved curatorially in the RA's 2009 *Earth: Art of a Changing World.*

*HEAT* was an essentially reflective rather than activist-based exhibition, prompting audiences to think critically about the modalities of climate change. Some of the projects commissioned especially for the exhibition were based on places and issues in and around Melbourne, thus providing relevance to local audiences. British artist Martin Reiser, for example, created an interactive multimedia video installation depicting and recording sounds from homes in the regional town of Bendigo. The viewer activates a scrolling streetscape as they move in front of the screen: upon pausing, stories from that house are triggered. All are about the extractive mining on which the town's economy historically relied and the more recent social and ecological impacts of the extended drought in the region.

According to its curator Linda Williams at the time, the exhibition "engages in a process of reflectivity that actively resists the emergence of a cultural regime of nostalgia arising from an impoverished world".[45] The goal of resisting sentimentality about ecosystem degeneration reveals a forward-looking curatorial intention to accept the new reality of a changed climate, an attitude that casts this exhibition in a similar category to *Radical Nature* and *In the Balance*. Like them, however (with the exception of *Dalston Mill*), while reflective and engaging, none of these exhibitions went that next step of proposing alternative, more environmentally sustainable relationships with the natural world.[46]

As echoed in the comments from the reviewer of *Radical Nature* in *Frieze* magazine and of *Earth: Art of a Changing World* in *The Spectator*, coming as they did from diametrically opposed political persuasions, even as recently as 2009–2010 art audiences were not ready to "learn" from, let alone deeply engage with, contemporary art premised on issues of climate change and ecological crisis. Just over a decade ago, the world was gradually becoming concerned with an imminent environmental crisis: in the 2020s it is upon us. It is useful therefore to compare the RA's environmental exhibition *Eco-Visionaries: Confronting a Planet in a State of Emergency* staged exactly ten years after *Earth* in 2019–2020.[47] As the curators stress, much changed over that decade:

> We are talking about the environment now more than ever before. Unprecedented coverage in newspapers, on social media and in prime-time documentaries is raising awareness of climate change, food consumption, resource depletion and species extinction. The demand for reusable water bottles, recyclable coffee cups, sustainable cotton clothing and biodegradable packaging is increasing exponentially. The number of people choosing a vegan diet has quadrupled since 2012.[48]

Unbeknown at the time of its planning and launch, *Eco-Visionaries* was to take place as bushfires ravaged eastern Australia, destroying over 30 million acres of bushland, leaving forest ecosystems destroyed and an estimated three billion native mammals, reptiles, birds, and frogs killed or injured and facing habitat loss, hunger, and predation.[49] At the same time, the COVID-19 pandemic was swiftly making its way from China to Europe, resulting in a protracted London lockdown that prompted the closure of the RA just three weeks after the exhibition finished in late February 2020. The relationship between bushfires and climate change is no longer disputed in Australia, and it has since been established by the scientific community that the COVID-19 pandemic is also a result of a human-propelled ecological crisis:

> As humans diminish biodiversity by cutting down forests and building more infrastructure, they're increasing the risk of disease pandemics such as COVID-19. . . while some species are going extinct, those that tend to survive and thrive – rats and bats, for instance – are more likely to host potentially dangerous pathogens that can make the jump to humans.[50]

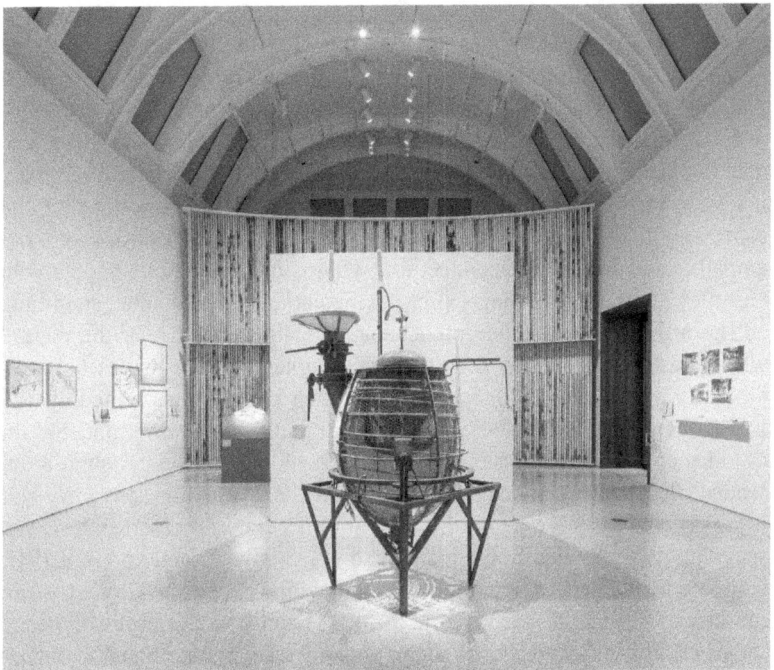

*Figure 1.3 Eco-Visionaries*, installation view, Royal Academy of Arts, London, 2019–2020. Foreground: SKREI, *Biogas Power Plant,* 2019.

Source: Courtesy and copyright Agnese Sanvito.

Photograph: Agnese Sanvito.

*Eco-Visionaries* sought to enlighten audiences about threats to biodiversity and to inspire action in the fields of art, design, and architecture to effect change. Elevating it from a passive art exhibition conveying mostly poetic or mournful responses to the demise of nature, *Eco-Visionaries* adopted a multidisciplinary platform, including projects by architects, artists, and designers whose practice addresses today's global ecological challenges. In contrast to exhibition writings for *Earth*, the curators of *Eco-Visionaries* ambitiously claimed that participants "propose inventive ways to tackle some of the world's most pressing issues of our time".[51] The exhibition also differed from *Earth* in its more confrontational, less meditative approach to the ecological crisis. This shift over the space of a decade to a more interdisciplinary, creative, and proactive stance on environmental issues signalled at the start of the 2020s a new era of curatorial endeavour designed to keep pace with fast-changing ecological crises and society's increasing appetite to solve them.

While well-intentioned and important as educational platforms, dissonance between curatorial intent and audience engagement risks undermining the impact of exhibitions such as this. This was clearly in evidence at the RA: the exhibition opened towards the end of the Academy's 2019 Antony Gormley survey exhibition, which in stark contrast to *Eco-Visionaries* was packed with viewers and opened for extended hours to accommodate demand. *Eco-Visionaries* was the more engaging exhibition on many levels – intellectually, scientifically, politically – but emotionally and especially in terms of the viewer experience, its creative proposals for more empathic and sustainable connections with nature could not compete with Gormley's visually arresting sculptural mediations on the human condition.

The artistic and audience preoccupation with the self over the natural world was exemplified by the antithetical topics of these two exhibitions, albeit for a brief ten-day overlap period. Their pairing transformed the RA into a microcosm of the social and political realities that have hindered for decades any meaningful global action on ecological crises. Though unintended, the thematic juxtaposition between the two exhibitions gave rise to a pertinent question about the direction of curatorial practice: how can speculative, scientifically premised, and essentially didactic presentations compete for audiences' attention with *Art* with a capital "A" by art world luminaries? There are lessons from the past. Land art was closely aligned to the beginnings of environmentalism, which for a curator attuned to changing socio-political views presented an opportunity to engage a broader section of the community in the concerns being voiced not just by artists but by a groundswell of ecologically aware members of the broader society. Environmental (land) art was artist led, at times facilitated and promoted by curators, borne out of research, passion, and a desire to make change.

A recent throwback to the ideological tenets of curating land art was staged in Berlin the following year. A rare, revolutionary example of an institution putting into practice its own rhetoric around environmental sustainability was an innovative exhibition in 2020 at Berlin's Gropius Bau. Like *Eco-Visionaries*, *Down to Earth* similarly embraced interdisciplinary practice and eschewed sentimentality, and to a large extent the pursuit of aesthetic pleasure. Further, reminiscent of the 1968–1969 land art exhibitions in the United States, it was unabashedly disruptive in purpose and austere in presentation, unusual for a major public art institution.

The exhibition adopted a curatorial methodology that put ambition into action. Radically for a museum setting, lead curator Thomas Oberender (director of Berlin Festspiele) committed to an "Unplugged" programme, embracing an expanded field of performative and participatory programmes. The power in the exhibition was unplugged to the letter: the lights and air-conditioning were turned off and the windows opened, no video or any artworks requiring electricity were included, and no air travel was permitted for the curators or participating artists.

The exhibition took its cue from Bruno Latour's eponymous essay on climate change.[52] Oberender adopted at face value Latour's contention that in order to survive, human society needs be brought back down to earth, to prioritise its place in the natural ecology over a disappearing dream of global solidarity. Investigating "how the agenda of a shift in climate policy affects our own 'operating system'", the curators drew on strategies championed by Claire Doherty's Situations and Bourriaud's *Relational Aesthetics*, aiming to turn the traditional museum exhibition model on its head by asking how curators can sustainably change how they work and make exhibitions.

> We want to play a different game. This isn't theatre, it's not an exhibition, not an exhibition with performances: it's something different. The whole thing is a situation. We open in the morning and close late. It's the summer. There will be things that you can see every day: objects, images, spatial installations – and four weeks of talks, lectures, dance and music changing every day.[53]

The result was an immersive environment, providing a hybrid experience reminiscent of being in a land art exhibition, an Apple store, an environmental seminar, and a performing arts venue. Visitors could choose their own level of engagement, and in some rooms the lack of natural lighting required the use of mobile phone flashlights to see the displays.

Asad Raza's *Absorption* comprising 20 tons of "neo-soil" was an echo of land art stretching back to Walter de Maria's *Earth Room* at Galerie

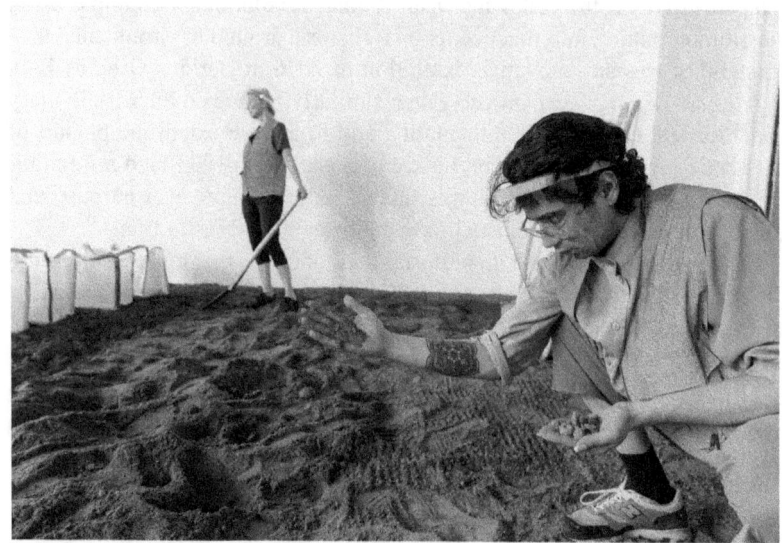

*Figure 1.4* Asad Raza, *Absorption*, 2020 (detail), *Down to Earth*, Gropius Bau, Berlin, 2020.

Source: Courtesy of the artist. Copyright Berliner Festspiele/Immersion.

Photograph: Eike Walkenhorst.

Heiner Friedrich, Munich, in 1968 (and later as an ephemeral intervention of soil scattered on the floor at the 1969 *Earth Art* exhibition at Cornell) and Helen Mayer Harrison and Newton Harrison's *Making Earth* of 1970. Like any soil, upon close inspection Raza's comprised many parts of a complex, life-giving ecosystem of which humans are part. Highlighting this interdependence, Raza's "soil" was made from the city's own ecosystem and contained barbeque ashes from a local park, grains of crushed stone and timber, and people's hair gathered from Berlin salons. Originally commissioned for Kaldor Art Projects in Sydney, Australia (2019), the positioning of people was understood as being within this ecosystem of "earth". Extending the sense of belonging as an intrinsic part of the ecosystem, visitors were handed bags of the material to take home.

Tino Sehgal was involved as both a curator and a participating artist (contributing a characteristic immaterial artwork), Russian artist and shaman Joulia Strauss celebrated Indigenous knowledges in *Rainbow Snake*, a soft

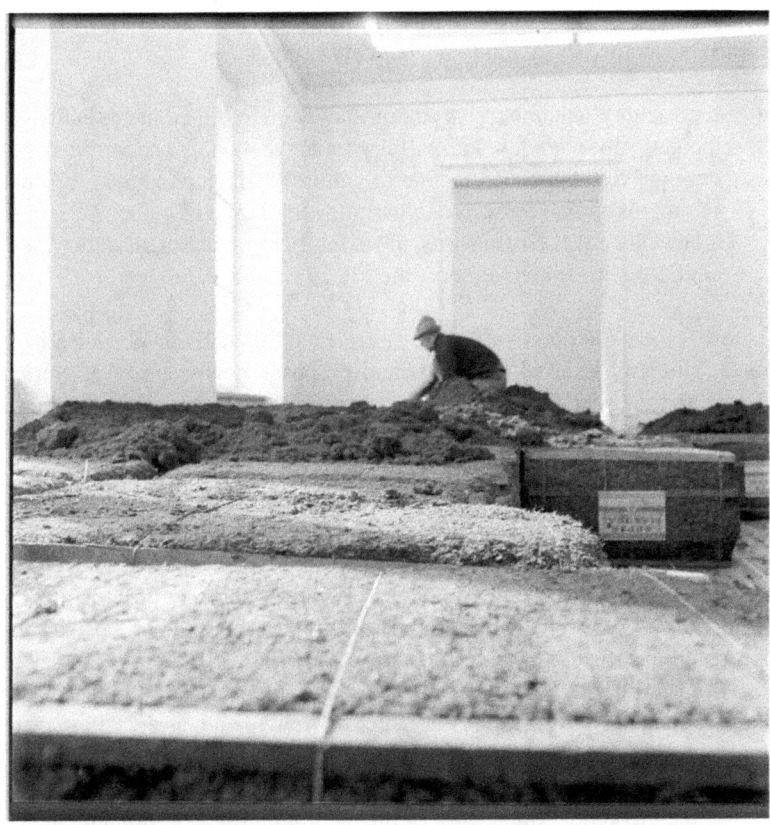

*Figure 1.5* Walter De Maria, *Earth Room*, Galerie Heiner Friedrich, München, 28.9.-10.10.1968.

Photograph: Heide Stolz © Nachlass Heide Stolz, DASMAXIMUM, Traunreut.

Source: ZADIK | Central Archive for German and International Art Market Research, University of Cologne, ZADIK Galerie Heiner Friedrich, A47, VIII, 1.

sculpture made from textiles, and Tomás Saraceno claimed as his artwork the spider webs that had gathered in the museum over preceding months. Reminiscent of the Barbican's *Dalston Mill* project, a structure exemplifying the efficiency of the "tiny house" movement was erected outdoors in collaboration with audience volunteers, from which electricity-free cooking and shared meals were undertaken. Like the MCA's *In the Balance* exhibition, there was an environmental audit of the exhibition itself.

The uncompromising commitment to austerity, engagement, and education was applauded by critics. Reviewer Sophia Bergmann, for example, clearly welcomed the exhibition's radical approach:

> It presents contemporary art that is daringly simplified in aesthetic, yet theoretically complex and wilfully unconventional. The world is not only viewed as a conglomerate of cultures and people, but as a planet of organisms that must live in harmony. In a time of global reflection, amidst the novel Coronavirus, the exhibition presents a set of new possibilities with which to reimagine life on Earth.[54]

Latour's thematic premise for the concurrent Taipei Biennale (see Chapter 2) similarly referred to planets and proposed new ways of inhabiting Earth, and the success of that biennale also depended largely on audience engagement both incidental and through a suite of innovative public programmes. Writing on Oberender's project, Dilpreet Bhullar claimed: "What makes this exhibition set apart from the spiking trends of exhibitions on climate change is the emphasis of the indigenous knowledge systems", her response also aligning with Latour's proposition that humans need to envisage themselves not as central to but as just one component of Earth's natural ecology: "The modes of sustainability hitherto pushed to the margins are resurrected to familiarise the audience with the available resources to reclaim the planet."[55] Bhullar's analysis of the Berlin exhibition is especially appreciative of the ways in which it drew in audiences, taking them on its journey of re-framing perceptions of our place in the world:

> If the theoretical framework of the exhibition revolves around climate change, it is the immersive experience that brings the audience a step closer to understand the gravity of the situation. Oberender declares, ". . . As we understand it, immersion consists of social rituals, scripted realities, creating opportunities for multisensory experiences in classically one-dimensional institutions – presenting music, dance, olfactory interventions, workshops, lectures etc. as natural programming in a traditional white cube environment. Ideally, we can push humanity being the centre of the world and all experience a little to one side and present a broader view of the ecology in which it is embedded, that is made up of machines, plants, social practices, other species and landscapes."

As a major museum-based exhibition, *Down to Earth* was an anomaly in the context of persistently traditional curatorial approaches to climate change and the ecological crisis by our museums and public art galleries. Large, public art institutions remain stubbornly risk averse for fear of disengaging not only audiences but the public, corporate, and philanthropic supporters that finance their programmes. *Down to Earth* was perhaps a harbinger of future directions, or, more likely, the one that was slipped through the wall (the museum is sited on the former Berlin Wall) by a sympathetic gatekeeper: Oberender had the support of Gropius Bau director Stephanie Rosenthal, appointed in 2017 on the strength of her creative approach as chief curator at London's Hayward Gallery (working with maverick curator Ralph Rugoff) and on the heels of her successful 2016 Biennale of Sydney, *The future is already here – it's just not evenly distributed*. When questioned about the funding controversy that preceded her appointment to the Biennale of Sydney, Rosenthal was adamant that "For me, it becomes impossible to work if there is censorship in what artists are allowed to say".[56] Rosenthal brought to the Gropius Bau the mindset of a biennale director who because of their inherently short-term tenure feels more able than a permanent staff member to advocate for their curators' and artists' visions.[57] It is this sense of liberty, unhindered by threats of institutional damage given their cyclical nature, that allows biennales to be less risk averse  than museums. Ideally, as this book argues, the biennale organisations themselves will similarly begin to embrace more radical experimentation as an ongoing commitment.

Although the origin of the curator's role is to "care" or "cure", very few public arts organisations are willing to literally switch off the lights to make an environmental statement. With the license to do so, however, Oberender embraced the opportunity to return to a time when curators championed care in both their exhibition-making and audiences. As he expressed in discussing the curators' aims for *Down to Earth*, "We want our visitors to come away with an experience of the world's richness . . . a blessing to us that brings with it a duty of care."[58]

Fifty years since the height of the land art movement, the current crisis faced by Earth is a mainstream preoccupation. In the 2020s, it is the voices of scientists that ring out most loudly, propelling people and more recently (some) politicians to take action. Unlike when Rachel Carson published *Silent Spring* in 1962 to the ire of most scientists, in 2022 art practice is echoing, rather than heralding, the conclusions of the scientific research confirming that the world is in a state of ecological crisis. Where land art succeeded in providing visual and experiential responses to environmental concerns at a time when the science was not being taken seriously, today's artists and curators are devising projects intended not simply to reflect and comment on the environment but to effect change in people's perception, understanding, and interaction with the natural environment. As the following chapters outline, it is often biennales, being agile international gatherings of ideas and relatively independent of restrictive institutional frameworks, that are leading the way.

Before investigating the curatorial experiments of biennales advancing more environmentally sustainable ways of living in the face of ecological crises, it is worth briefly acknowledging that visual arts programmes initiated by non-art recurrent international events and gatherings can also impact audiences' understanding of the climate crisis. Most specifically, the annual Conference of the Parties (COP) international convention, also known as the United Nations Climate Change Conference, has since its inaugural meeting in 1995 hosted parallel cultural events in each host city. These have been environmentally themed presentations, mostly taking the form of visual art exhibitions including screenings, data visualisations, and installations.

*Earth: Art of a Changing World* at the RA was timed to coincide with that year's United Nations Climate Change Conference (2009), one that optimistically set out to establish an ambitious global climate agreement, but in the lead up reduced its aims to instead reach some kind of politically binding agreement, and in the end is remembered as a spectacular failure to do either. The exhibition was not part of the official programme of cultural offerings in Copenhagen but an independent initiative by the RA that nevertheless succeeded in maximising interest from the public due to the COP15 conference receiving widespread media coverage.

Of the official cultural programmes to date, it is the 2015 COP21 suite of exhibitions in Paris that offered some of the more impactful visual arts projects. These included the physically immersive and profoundly affecting data visualisation of impending climate change and resulting societal catastrophe. Created by New York based design studio Dillier Scofido + Renfro based on data on the increasing preponderance of environmental disasters, sea level rises, population shifts, forced migration, and economic inequality, it is a work of compelling persuasion in its urgent call for climate action and has since been shown in China, Australia, and across the United States. COP21 also commissioned major installations from leading contemporary artists including Janet Laurence (Australia) and the late Naziha Mestaoui (Belgium), both artists known for their commitment to knowledge transfer through installations designed to immerse the viewer rendered natural environments. Mestaoui's *One Tree, One Planet* light installation was projected onto some of the city's landmarks during the conference, transforming the Eiffel Tower, Arc de Triomphe, and Hotel de Ville into virtual forests. For the 2022 Biennale of Sydney, another of her "tree of life" projects will be posthumously reimagined to be in dialogue with the concurrently reinstated iteration of Joseph Beuys' *7000 Oaks* in that city.[59]

The disappointing 2021 COP26 conference had an even more urgent set of targets in light of the IPCC's dire warnings issued in the report just months before the Glasgow conference. Bringing together a range of exhibitions and related programmes, *Climate Beacons for COP26* was a Scotland-wide collaborative project between climate change and environmental organisations and arts, heritage, and cultural organisations. Run by arts and sustainability initiative Creative Carbon Scotland, the aim was to promote greater collaboration between the cultural and climate sectors, and stimulate public engagement around and following the UN climate talks in late 2021.[60] As programme lead Lewis Coenen-Rowe explains, "The arts offer empathetic, subjective, and fantastical ways of engaging with climate change that we as humans need and that are hard to find space for in traditional forms of climate change public engagement."[61]

Increasingly today, we are seeing the soft power of visually and socially engaging art practices to advance dialogue and awareness around environmental issues manifest not just in one-off, artist-led projects but in major public events and exhibitions, as curators utilise the high profile status of events such as biennales to challenge the status quo, propose alternatives, and facilitate knowledge transfer. These new curatorial approaches are the result of a sense of urgency: when land art was established as a new and viable genre of contemporary art in the 1960s and 1970s, despite the groundswell of environmental awareness, exhibitions were not then being (consciously) curated in a time of ecological crisis.

## Notes

1 *The Stern Review on the Economics of Climate Change* (UK, 2006) and *The Garnaut Climate Change Review* (Australia, 2008).
2 Agnes Denes, *Wheatfield – A Confrontation*, Manhattan, 1982; Alan Sonfist, *Time Landscape*, Manhattan, 1978; Joseph Beuys, *7000 Oaks: City Forestation Instead of City Administration*, documenta, Kassel, 1982.
3 Michael Heizer, *Dragged Mass Displacement*, Detroit, Detroit Institute of Arts, 1971. See pp. 19–20.
4 While the phenomenon of global warming was recognised by scientists as early as the 1930s (see the work of British engineer Guy Stewart Callendar, for example), the first time that the term "global warming" was used in the title and was the dedicated subject of a scientific paper on the topic was in 1975 by American geochemist Wallace Broecker. See Richard Black, "A Brief History of Climate Change", 20 September 2013, www.bbc.com/news/science-environment-15874560 (accessed 1 November 2020).
5 Linda Lear, "Introduction", in *Silent Spring: The Classic that Launched the Environmental Movement*, New York, Mariner Books, 2002, p. xi.
6 Phillip Kaiser and Miwon Kwon, "Ends of the Earth and Back", in *Ends of the Earth: Land Art to 1974*, Los Angeles, The Museum of Contemporary Art, 2012, p. 19.
7 Kaiser and Kwon, "Ends of the Earth and Back".
8 Kaiser and Kwon, "Ends of the Earth and Back", p. 93.

9  The projects were staged by Siegelaub at Bradfield College, Massachusetts, in February, 1968 and Windham College in Putney, Vermont, in April, 1968. The same three artists participated in both: Carl Andre, Robert Barry and Lawrence Weiner.

10 The first occurrence of the term "land art" was Gerry Schum's use of it in his 1969 film of the same name. Kaiser and Kwon, "Ends of the Earth and Back", p. 17.

11 "Willoughby Sharp" (interview). Kaiser and Kwon, "Ends of the Earth and Back", p. 38.

12 Bruce Altshuler, "Introduction", in *Biennials and Beyond – Exhibitions That Made Art History*, London, Phaidon Press, 2013, p. 15.

13 Olafur Eliasson and Minik Rosing, *Ice Watch,* 2014. For a discussion of the Heizer case, see Paul Martineaux, *The Thrill of the Chase: The Wagstaff Collection of Photographs at the J. Paul Getty Museum*, Los Angeles, Getty Publications, 2016, p. 9.

14 Haeg's *Edible Estates* project saw the establishment of fruit and vegetable gardens in several sites across the United States and one in London, commissioned by Tate Modern in 2007. See Diana Balmori (ed.), *Edible Estates: Attack on the Front Lawn*, Texas, Bellerophon Publications Inc., 2008.

15 While 60 percent of the trees planted by 1987 were varieties of oak, other species were incorporated into the project. Fifteen other tree species were used. They include ash, chestnut, crab, elm, gingko, hawthorn, locust, maple, and walnut. Lynne Cooke, "Joseph Beuys – 7000 Oaks", http://web.mit.edu/allanmc/www/cookebeuys.pdf (accessed 31 May 2019).

16 Stefan Körner and Florian Bellin-Harder, "The 7000 Eichen of Joseph Beuys – Experiences after Twenty-Five Years", *Journal of Landscape Architecture*, vol. 4, no. 2, 2009.

17 Cook (unpaginated). Other species planted to date by Dia include Bradford callery pear, common hackberry, ginkgo, japanese pagoda, japanese zelkova, littleleaf linden, pin oak, sycamore, and thornless honey locust.

18 Conversations with Leon Paroissien, Sydney, 21 February and 4 June, 2019.

19 Susanna Byrne, "Interview with Acroyd & Harvey" (originally commissioned by Silent City Collective in reaction to the Royal Academy's exhibition *Earth: Art of a Changing World, This Is Tomorrow*), 24 July, 2010, http://thisistomorrow.info/articles/susanna-byrne-talks-to-ackroyd-harvey (accessed 3 June 2019).

20 The Asia Pacific Triennial at Queensland Art Gallery and Gallery of Modern Art was established in 1993 and the NGV Triennial at the National Gallery of Victoria in 2017.

21 Biennale of Sydney board meeting minutes 16 February, 1979, Biennale of Sydney Archive, Art Gallery of New South Wales Library.

22 Fujiko Nakaya, *Earth Talk*. Exhibited 1976 Biennale of Sydney. Installed as *Foggy wake in a desert: An ecosphere*, Canberra, National Gallery of Australia, 1982.

23 Mark Boyle, *Studies of Cliffs and Desert Terrain, Central Australian Desert*, Exhibited 1979 Biennale of Sydney.

24 Joseph Beuys in conversation with Richard DeMarco. Martin John Haigha, "Connective Practices in Sustainability Education", *Journal of Applied Technical and Educational Sciences*, vol. 7, no. 4, 2017, pp. 11–12.

25 Matthew Gandy, "Contradictory Modernities: Conceptions of Nature in the Art of Joseph Beuys and Gerhard Richter", *Annals of the Association of American Geographers*, vol. 87, no. 4, 1997, pp. 641–644.

26 Conversations with Leon Paroissien, Sydney, 21 February and 4 June, 2019.
27 Anonymous, *Moreton Bay Fig: History*, New South Wales Office of Environment & Heritage, www.environment.nsw.gov.au/heritageapp/ViewHeritage ItemDetails.aspx?ID=2700766 (accessed 10 June 2019).
28 Conversations with Leon Paroissien, Sydney, 21 February and 4 June, 2019.
29 Bernice Murphy, *Notes Sent to Andrew Andersons [Architect] to Explain the Significance of the 'Beuys Fig Tree' Near the Art Gallery of New South Wales*, 23 March 2018 (unpublished, shared by the author). In contrast to Sydney, however, in Kassel, all 7,000 basalt stones were deposited in front of the Museum Fridericianum with the intention that the pile would diminish as each one was removed to accompany a newly planted tree.
30 Conversations with Leon Paroissien, Sydney, 21 February and 4 June, 2019.
31 Nicholas Stern et al., *The Stern Review on the Economics of Climate Change*, 30 October, 2006. N.H. Stern, *The Economics of Climate Change: The Stern Review,* Cambridge, Cambridge University Press, 2007.
32 Nicolas Bourriaud, *Relational Aesthetics*, Dijon, Les Presses du Réel, 2002.
33 Stephen Beasley, "Radical Nature", *Frieze* (Reviews), no. 126, October, 2009, www.frieze.com/article/radical-nature-art-and-architecture-changing-planet-1969–2009 (accessed 10 November 2020).
34 It was not the first seminal project from the environmental art movement in the early 1980s to be revisited in the 21st century: as discussed earlier, Joseph Beuys' *7000 Oaks* was curated into the Biennale of Sydney at the time, lost and forgotten, then relaunched as part of the new Sydney Modern building project undertaken by the Art Gallery of NSW in 2020–2022.
35 Exyst – *Dalston Mill,* https://vimeo.com/5541507 (accessed 10 August 2021).
36 Fraser Nelson, "Earth: Art of a Changing World", *The Spectator*, 5 January, 2010, www.studiointernational.com/index.php/gsk-contemporary-earth-art-of-a-changing-world (accessed 21 May 2021).
37 https://capefarewell.com/art/past-projects/earth-art-of-a-changing-world.html (accessed 20 May 2021).
38 https://capefarewell.com/art/past-projects/earth-art-of-a-changing-world.html (accessed 20 May 2021).
39 Susan Norrie and David McKenzie, *Havoc*, 16-channel video, 2007, commissioned by the Australia Council for the Arts for the 52nd Biennale of Venice, 2007.
40 Rachel Kent, "Introduction", in *In the Balance: Art for a Changing World*, Sydney, Museum of Contemporary Art, 2010, p. 15.
41 The works included: The Artist as Family, *Food Forest*; Diego Bonetto, *5 terraariums, 5 tours and a world of Facebook friends*; Joni Taylor, *Wildlife in the City: Urban Wildlife Safari*; and Jeanne van Heeswijk, *Talking Trash – Personal Relationships with Waste*. The community-based project by van Heeswijk was originally commissioned by MCA Senior Curator Anne Loxely as part of the MCA's C3West programme (2010).
42 T.J. Demos, "The Politics of Sustainability: Art and Ecology", in Francesco Manacorda (ed.), *Radical Nature: Art and Architecture for a Changing Planet, 1969–2009*, Köln, Walther König, 2009, pp. 16–30.
43 Glenn Barkley and Lucas Ihlein, "Lucas Ihlein: Environmental Audit", in Rachel Kent (ed.), "Introduction", p. 102.
44 See Chapter 3 for a discussion of this project.

45  Linda Williams, "Reshaping the Human Self Image: Contemporary Art & Climate Change", in Suzanne Davies (ed.), *HEAT: Art and Climate Change*, Melbourne, RMIT Gallery, 2008, p. 14.

46  Earlier in 2008, one of three thematic strands in Australia's national biennale was climate change and included works by artists later shown in *HEAT*. See Felicity Fenner (curator and editor), *Handle with Care: 2008 Biennial of Australian Art*, Adelaide, Art Gallery of South Australia, 2008.

47  Eco-Visionaries is the collective title of an international curatorial endeavour between museums in Portugal, Sweden, Switzerland, Spain, and the UK. Participating organisations were Fundação EDP/MAAT (Museum of Art, Architecture and Technology, Lisbon, Portugal), Bildmuseet (Umeå, Sweden), HeK (House of Electronic Arts, Basel, Switzerland) and LABoral (Gijón, Spain), in collaboration with the Royal Academy of Arts (London, UK) and Matadero Madrid (Madrid, Spain).

48  Gonzalo Herrero Delicado and Rose Thompson, "On a Planetary Emergency", in Gonzalo Herrero et al. (eds.), *Eco-Visionaries: Conversations on a Planet in a State of Emergency*, London, Royal Academy Publications, 2019, pp. 9–10.

49  Lily M. van Eeden et al., *Impacts of the Unprecedented 2019–2020 Bushfires on Australian Animals*, Sydney, Report prepared for WWF-Australia, 2020.

50  Jeff Tollefson, "Why Deforestation and Extinctions Make Pandemics More Likely", *Nature*, 7 August, 2020, www.nature.com/articles/d41586-020-02341-1 (accessed 23 May 2021).

51  Tollefson, "Why Deforestation and Extinctions Make Pandemics More Likely", p. 15.

52  Bruno Latour, *Down to Earth: Politics in the New Climatic Regime*, Hoboken, NJ, Wiley, 2018.

53  Thomas Oberender, Exhibition Guide, "Down to Earth", 2020, www.berliner festspiele.de/en/berliner-festspiele/programm/bfs-gesamtprogramm/program mdetail_309206.html (accessed 20 June 2021).

54  Sophia Bergmann, "Achieving Latour's Terrestrial Down to Earth at Gropius Bau", *Berlin Art Link*, 25 August, 2020, www.berlinartlink.com/2020/08/25/achieving-latours-terrestrial-down-to-earth-at-gropius-bau/ (accessed 22 June 2021).

55  Dilpreet Bhullar, "Multi-Sensory Experience of Down to Earth Underlines Efficacy of Collective Action", *Stirworld*, 3 September, 2020, www.stirworld.com/see-features-multi-sensory-experience-of-down-to-earth-underlines-efficacy-of-collective-action (accessed 22 June 2021).

56  Andrew Taylor, "Sydney Biennale 2016: Big, Brash and Still Grappling with Refugees and Migration", *Sydney Morning Herald*, 9 March, 2016, www.smh.com.au/entertainment/art-and-design/sydney-biennale-2016-big-brash-and-still-grappling-with-refugees-and-migration-20160307-gncl5e.html (accessed 3 July 2021).

57  Hou Hanru, director of Rome's MAXXI, similarly brings the mindset of a biennale director to curating in the context of a major museum.

58  Bhullar, "Multi-Sensory Experience".

59  Conversation with Jose Roca, 2 May, 2021, Sydney.

60  Lewis Coenen-Rowe, " 'Climate Beacons' to Bring Together Culture and Green Sectors for COP26", *Creative Carbon Scotland*, 29 March, 2021, www.crea tivescotland.com/what-we-do/latest-news/archive/2021/03/climate-beacons-for-cop26 (accessed 15 August 2021).

61  Correspondence with the author, 25 August, 2021.

## Bibliography

Altshuler, Bruce, "Introduction", In *Biennials and Beyond – Exhibitions That Made Art History*, London, Phaidon Press, 2013.

Author unspecified, "Earth: Art of a Changing World". https://capefarewell.com/art/past-projects/earth-art-of-a-changing-world.html

Author unspecified, *Moreton Bay Fig: History*, New South Wales Office of Environment & Heritage. www.environment.nsw.gov.au/heritageapp/ViewHeritageItem Details.aspx?ID=2700766

Balmori, Diana (ed.), *Edible Estates: Attack on the Front Lawn*, Texas, Bellerophon Publications Inc., 2008.

Beasley, Stephen, "Radical Nature", *Frieze* (Reviews), no. 126, October, 2009. www.frieze.com/article/radical-nature-art-and-architecture-changing-planet-1969-2009

Bergmann, Sophia, "Achieving Latour's Terrestrial Down to Earth at Gropius Bau", *Berlin Art Link*, 25 August, 2020. www.berlinartlink.com/2020/08/25/achieving-latours-terrestrial-down-to-earth-at-gropius-bau/

Bhullar, Dilpreet, "Multi-Sensory Experience of Down to Earth Underlines Efficacy of Collective Action", *Stirworld*, 3 September, 2020. www.stirworld.com/see-features-multi-sensory-experience-of-down-to-earth-underlines-efficacy-of-collective-action

Biennale of Sydney board meeting minutes 16 February, 1979, Biennale of Sydney Archive, Art Gallery of New South Wales Library.

Black, Richard, "A Brief History of Climate Change", 20 September, 2013. www.bbc.com/news/science-environment-15874560

Bourriaud, Nicolas, *Relational Aesthetics*, Dijon, Les Presses du Réel, 2002.

Byrne, Susanna, "Interview with Acroyd & Harvey" (originally commissioned by Silent City Collective in reaction to the Royal Academy's exhibition *Earth: Art of a Changing World*), *This is Tomorrow*, 24 July, 2010. http://thisistomorrow.info/articles/susanna-byrne-talks-to-ackroyd-harvey

Coenen-Rowe, Lewis, " 'Climate Beacons' to Bring Together Culture and Green Sectors for COP26", *Creative Carbon Scotland*, 29 March, 2021. www.creativescotland.com/what-we-do/latest-news/archive/2021/03/climate-beacons-for-cop26

Cooke, Lynne, "Joseph Beuys – 7000 Oaks". http://web.mit.edu/allanmc/www/cookebeuys.pdf

Davies, Suzanne (ed.), *HEAT: Art and Climate Change*, Melbourne, RMIT Gallery Exyst, "The Dalston Mill". https://vimeo.com/5541507

Gandy, Matthew, "Contradictory Modernities: Conceptions of Nature in the Art of Joseph Beuys and Gerhard Richter", *Annals of the Association of American Geographers*, vol. 87, no. 4, 1997, pp. 641–644.

Haigha, Martin John, "Connective Practices in Sustainability Education", *Journal of Applied Technical and Educational Sciences*, vol. 7, no. 4, 2017, pp. 11–12.

Herrero Delicado, Gonzalo et al. (eds.), *Eco-Visionaries: Conversations on a Planet in a State of Emergency*, London, Royal Academy Publications, 2019.

Kaiser, Phillip and Miwon Kwon, "Ends of the Earth and Back", In *Ends of the Earth: Land Art to 1974*, Los Angeles, The Museum of Contemporary Art, 2012.

Kent, Rachel (ed.), *In the Balance: Art for a Changing World*, Sydney, Museum of Contemporary Art, 2010.

Körner, Stefan and Florian Bellin-Harder, "The 7000 Eichen of Joseph Beuys – Experiences after Twenty-Five Years", *Journal of Landscape Architecture*, vol. 4, no. 2, 2009.

Latour, Bruno, *Down to Earth: Politics in the New Climatic Regime*, Hoboken, NJ, Wiley, 2018.

Lear, Linda (ed.), *Silent Spring: The Classic that Launched the Environmental Movement*, New York, Mariner Books, 2002.

Manacorda, Francesco (ed.), *Radical Nature: Art and Architecture for a Changing Planet, 1969–2009*, Köln, Walther König, 2009.

Martineaux, Paul, *The Thrill of the Chase: The Wagstaff Collection of Photographs at the J. Paul Getty Museum*, Los Angeles, Getty Publications, 2016.

Nelson, Fraser, "Earth: Art of a Changing World", *The Spectator*, 5 January, 2010. www.studiointernational.com/index.php/gsk-contemporary-earth-art-of-a-changing-world

Oberender, Thomas, "Exhibition Guide", In *Down to Earth*, 2020. www.berliner festspiele.de/en/berliner-festspiele/programm/bfs-gesamtprogramm/program mdetail_309206.html

Obrist, Hans Ulrich and Kostas Stasinopoulos, *140 Artists' Ideas for Planet Earth*, London, Serpentine Galleries, 2021.

Stern, Nicholas et al., *The Stern Review on the Economics of Climate Change*, 2006.

N.H. Stern, *The Economics of Climate Change: The Stern Review*, Cambridge, Cambridge University Press, 2007.

Taylor, Andrew, "Sydney Biennale 2016: Big, Brash and Still Grappling with Refugees and Migration", *Sydney Morning Herald*, 9 March, 2016. www.smh.com. au/entertainment/art-and-design/sydney-biennale-2016-big-brash-and-still-grap pling-with-refugees-and-migration-20160307-gncl5e.html

Tollefson, Jeff, "Why Deforestation and Extinctions Make Pandemics More Likely", *Nature*, 7 August, 2020. www.nature.com/articles/d41586-020-02341-1

van Eeden Lily, M. Dale Nimmo, Michael Mahony, Kerryn Herman, Glenn Ehmke, Joris Driessen, James O'Connor, Gilad Bino, Martin Taylor and Chris Dickman, *Impacts of the Unprecedented 2019–2020 Bushfires on Australian Animals*, 2020. Report prepared for WWF-Australia, 2020.

# 2    Critical Ecosystems

## Biennales and New Curatorial Strategies in Response to Climate Change

As the urgency of addressing the world's climate crisis became mainstream news following COP21 and the resulting 2016 Paris Agreement, curators in many parts of the world conceived environmentally themed, cohesive exhibitions that transformed traditional museum or similar indoor spaces into ecosystems that reflected the interconnectedness of the natural world. At the 2019 Venice Biennale alone, for example, at least eight national pavilions staged exhibitions that directly addressed the impacts of climate change, including particularly strong works by Laure Provoust in the French pavilion and by the Finnish, Norwegian, and Swedish artists in the Nordic Countries pavilion.

Biennales differ from other large exhibitions in their inherent capacity to respond with agility to issues of the moment. For this reason, biennales are well positioned to provide a compelling snapshot of prevailing social preoccupations. This chapter looks at recent biennales that were curated in response to the ecological crisis and successfully reimagined traditional exhibition spaces such as museums and galleries to create discrete ecosystems referencing those found in nature. The curatorial strategies and exhibitions' success in fostering interdisciplinary research and audience engagement are discussed in relation to the 2019 Lyon Biennale, the 2020–2021 EVA International Biennial of Contemporary Art in Limerick, and both the 2018 and 2020 editions of the Taipei Biennial.

In applauding curatorial attempts to address complex environmental issues, it is important to concede that most curators, like the artists whose work they represent, are not in pole position to save the planet. Curators lack scientific training and the informed understanding of scientific facts that it affords. The consequence of basing exhibitions and creative works on a superficial comprehension of the complexities of ecological crises can lead to perceptions of catastrophising or pontificating, or, at the other end of the spectrum, a tendency to sugar-coat the dire environmental situation

DOI: 10.4324/9781003130574-3

confronting the planet. The first option risks disengaging audiences who recognise the work as alarmist and indoctrinating; the second can belittle the seriousness of the future we are facing in its pretence that artworks and individual viewers can make any measurable impact on achieving less disastrous outcomes than those predicted by the scientific community.

While most of the eco-focused biennales in recent years are premised on commonly accepted scientific knowledge, not all biennales subscribe to its somewhat pessimistic outlook. The curatorial premise of the 2019 Triennale de Milano, an architecture biennale, proposed a silver lining in the face of gloom: "Humans will inevitably become extinct due to environmental breakdown, but we have the power to design ourselves a 'beautiful ending'", claiming the Triennale could be "the beginning of people talking about the reality in a positive way".[1] Also in 2019, the relatively small-scale Manif d'art – Quebec City Biennial in Canada rejected bleak perspectives on the climate crisis. Instead, curator Jonathan Watkins explored questions about humans' relationship to natural environments in ways that were philosophical rather than driven by a sense of alarm. "Far from being pessimistic, the artists reveal their observations, ideas, fixations and utopias, whether they're metaphorical, playful, political or poetic."[2]

One work that did not tow the exhibition's reflective line was a dystopian installation of discarded computers, cables, adapters, and batteries by Czech artist Kristof Kintera. Commenting on the environmentally reckless culture of hyperconsumption and planned obsolescence, the elements spread like toxic triffids across the floor of the gallery, evoking the destructive underbelly of modern technology. Kintera's installation brought an edgy sensibility and quirky imagining to the Québec Biennial, a dark, post-apocalyptic aesthetic that informed the Lyon Biennial later that year.

In 2019, the world's attention to the many ecological crises unfolding in the face of global climate change reached a highpoint. In January the teenaged Swedish environmental activist Greta Thunberg addressed world leaders at the World Economic Forum, telling them that "our house is on fire" and beseeching them not to offer hope but to panic and act with the urgency that is required.[3] Later in 2019 the School Strike for Climate movement, which had begun the previous year with Thunberg's lonely protest outside the Swedish Riksdag, went global with millions of people participating in rolling strikes led by school children across the world.

## 2019 Lyon Biennale

Curators already supporting and presenting art inspired by ecological issues were propelled by the growing momentum of environmental action, seizing the opportunity in what may have been the start of an environmental turn in contemporary curatorial practice had not COVID-19 swiftly caused the art world to screech to a halt in early 2020. One of the last cabs off the pre-pandemic biennale rank was the 2019 Lyon Biennale of Contemporary Art. Attuned to a global public concerned with ecological crises in addition to a local economy adversely impacted by globalisation, the exhibition was notable for its success in shifting the curatorial emphasis away from philosophical reflection or crude protest, instead creating an ecosystem exploring human and post-human relationships with natural and manufactured environments.

Titled *Where Water Comes Together with Other Water*, the 2019 Lyon Biennale captured the public spirit for urgent change as the American election loomed, and with it the possibility of a turnaround from apathy to action on global environmental programmes. Through the metaphor of water, it explored ideas around the flow and flux of work and labour and more overtly environmental and biological metamorphosis in the face of rapidly changing climatic conditions. The resource-intensive habit of importing large-scale artworks from different corners of the globe was dispensed with, as half the artists were European and a third of them French. The downside of this was an exhibition largely devoid of cultural diversity. The huge advantage and innovation, however, was that by relying on local knowledge and expertise the biennale demonstrated how a local system of networks can offer a successful eco-sustainable response to the need for large exhibitions such as biennales to address the climate crisis not just in conceptual but in practical ways.

Lyon's biennale was launched in 1991 by Thierry Raspail, founding director since 1984 of the Musée d'art contemporain de Lyon (macLYON). After curating the first three editions, Raspail delegated curatorial oversight to invited international curators including Harald Szeemann, Hans Ulrich Obrist, Nicolas Bourriaud, Hou Hanru, Ralph Rugoff, and Emma Lavigne. Despite well-known international curators being appointed, Raspail maintained the title of artistic director and provided the conceptual starting point for each edition.[4] Raspail's retirement in 2018 from his roles as both director of macLYON and artistic director of the biennale, and appointment of macLYON exhibitions director Isabelle Bertolotti to the roles, offered a timely opportunity for a new curatorial model to be introduced. Bertolotti's appointment of curators from the Palais de Tokyo signalled a new direction, with the biennale being curated for the first time by a team, comprising outgoing Palais de Tokyo director Jean de Loisy and seven younger-generation curators.[5]

The 15th Lyon Biennale opened in September 2019 and ended in January 2020, by which time COVID-19 was already but unknowingly circulating in France. Less than two months after its closure, the pandemic lockdowns began. This new reality of being confined to a narrow geographic area forced a similar reliance on and appreciation of local potential and production as that espoused by the biennale. In an unanticipated case of art presaging life, the biennale enabled an unusually high proportion – almost half the exhibition content – not only to be site-specific but to be fabricated in Lyon, taking into account the socio-economic context of the works' production and presentation. This was a commitment made by the new artistic director on the basis of environmental sustainability and also of fostering engagement with local audiences:

> With this edition we have wanted to support the creation of new works in a wide variety of forms of expression and with connections to local means of production . . . encouraging fluidity between fields of expression, a heterogeneous public and a wide variety of venues . . . in tune with both local and international concerns.[6]

The biennale's first multi-curator team conceived of the exhibition as growing out of Lyon itself, both thematically and practically. Amid growing international scepticism around the carbon footprint of biennales, they were keen to test a new, more environmentally and economically sustainable exhibition model that also supported its community by leveraging local knowledge and production.

Conceptually, the exhibition was rigorous. The title, taken from a Raymond Carver poem, was appropriately themed to Lyon, located at the confluence of the Rhône and Saône rivers. The largest of the two main exhibitions comprising the biennale was at the abandoned Fagor factory, which used to manufacture home appliances, most notably heavy-duty washing machines designed for hotels and laundromats. A handful of artists' projects were exhibited at macLYON, but they felt disconnected both from each other and from the thematic coherence of the much more engaging exhibition at the Fagor factory.

Lyon is historically an industrial powerhouse, a hub for many and diverse industries from textiles and metals to, in the second half of the 20th century, automobile, chemical, and biotech industries. The Fagor factory is for locals a well-known landmark on an 11-acre site in the working-class Gerland district of the city. It was operational until 2015, so is still very much in the memory of the local community, many of whom either worked or had family members employed at the facility. Given the social impact of the area's post-industrial regeneration, which has seen a substantial downturn in availability of the manufacturing jobs that once sustained its population, biennale organisers felt duty bound to redistribute the event's 10 million euro budget among the regional population.[7] This was achieved by employing for the fabrication of artworks labourers in the region made redundant through factory closures or otherwise unemployed. Like Japan's Echigo-Tsumari Triennale with its active (though volunteer based) involvement of mostly retired farmers (see Chapter 3), this approach fostered a circular economy, situating the Lyon Biennale as an active participant in the community and meaningful contributor to its socio-economic wellbeing.

The Fagor factory is massive in scale, its soaring ceilings and vestiges of industrial infrastructure, old machinery, and human labour offering a similar backdrop to the exhibition as Sydney's Cockatoo Island, or, in its early, rawer days, Venice's Arsenale. Like those biennale venues, the spectacle of the cavernous spaces, with their remnant objects and traces of human activity from a different socio-economic context and other time, often competed with the artworks for attention. In their catalogue introduction, the curators ambitiously asserted that the space within the factory

> has been transformed, thanks to the works exhibited in it, into an anthropogenic ecosystem at the intersection of biological, economic and cosmogonic landscapes . . . in which artworks that affect neither apocalyptic discourse nor an aesthetic of disaster, nor seek to romanticise ruins, bear witness to shifting relationships between humans and non-humans, the living and the non-living.[8]

The theme of interconnection between bodies, objects, and spaces was manifest throughout the exhibition in site-specific installations that, despite the claim of sidestepping apocalyptic narratives, created an enveloping end-of-the world visual and visceral experience. Disturbing and anthropomorphic installations were created from textile, chemical, and industrial components, materials emblematic of Lyon's manufacturing history.

Convincing in the context of conceptualising eco-sustainable futures was the exhibition's staging of "new narratives with multiple geographies and temporalities that testify to fluctuating and precarious arrangements with our contemporaries".[9] One of the first works to confront viewers was Italian artist Nico Vascellari's collection of life-size wax-sculpted animals mounted sideways onto car engines. They appropriated animals just as the once-prominent Lyonnaise automobile industry did as trademarks, arranged in a macabre conjoining with car engines, the works emphasising the awkward and unnatural merging of animal and machine. Just beyond this installation, South African artist Simphiwe Ndzube presented a carnival-like procession of bloated, faceless human figures clad in collaged textiles resembling both mythological and contemporary clothing. The figures were clearly workers of some kind, some spiritual in presentation and others gravediggers equipped with shovels, symbolically shepherding the group from one world to another.

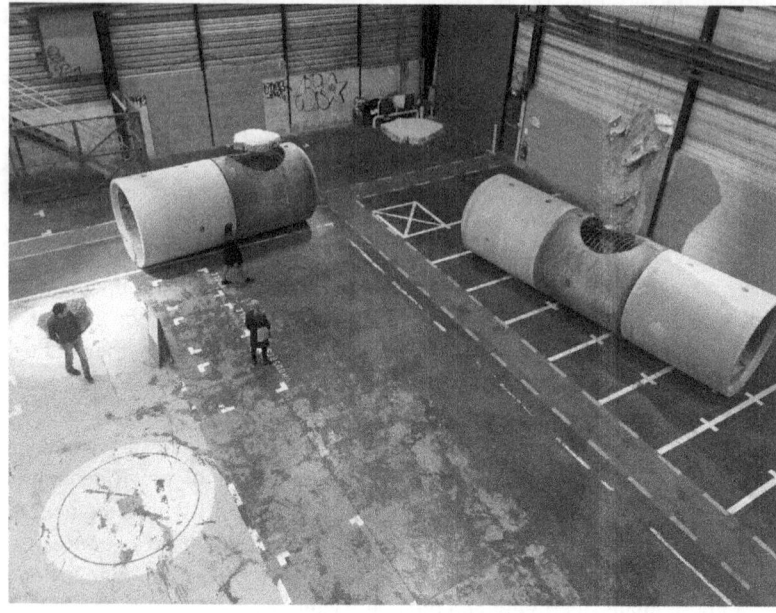

*Figure 2.1* Fagor Factory, installation view, Lyon Biennale, 2019, showing Panna-
phan Yodmanee, *Quarterly Myth*, 2019.

Photograph: Felicity Fenner.

Works in this first, largest space of the Fagor factory by Rebecca Ackroyd
(UK), Stéphanie Thidet (France), and Megan Rooney (Canada) similarly
conflated natural and industrial references in anthropomorphic installations
that conveyed violence, pain, and loss. Elsewhere, Thomas Feurerstein
(Austria) and Léonard Martin (France) borrowed iconic figurative imagery
from European art history, specifically an 18th-century depiction of the
Greek god Prometheus and Paolo Uccello's paintings of medieval battles.
In different ways they dematerialised bodily representations, proposing
an alternative, post-human relationship to the Fagor factory and the world
more broadly.

The third dominating curatorial theme in the Lyon Biennale was exemplified in works by Isabelle Andriessen (Netherlands) and Bianca Bondi
(South Africa), installations premised on alchemical entanglements with the
concrete and atmospheric aura of the factory itself. With unintended presci-
ence as COVID-19 seeped its way into our lives, Andriessen's installation,
made from inanimate materials such as epoxy and aluminium, was designed
to "melt and metabolise" over the duration of the exhibition as the materials

reacted with the post-industrial environment: "The sculptures behave like organisms infected by a strange virus or like eerie mutants from a hypothetical future. They are parasitic . . . an unsettling and speculative ecosystem that moves beyond control."[10]

Bondi's work transformed a former kitchen space into a laboratory for experimentation involving "constantly mutating ecosystems that evolve through her chemical operations and a sprinkling of magic, assisted by the moon's powers and the purifying properties of salt".[11] Surfaces were encrusted with a thick layer of salt and domestic vessels filled with liquids of various colour that changed over the course of the Biennale. The chemistry inherent to both installations references the prevalence of that industry in Lyon, as well as the Biennale's themes of confluence and metamorphosis.

While individual works such as these at the Fagor factory (but less so the presentation at macLYON) supported the curators' aim to create an "anthropogenic ecosystem at the intersection of biological, economic and cosmogonic landscapes", the real success of the biennale was its forging of new production models.[12] The commitment to and utilisation of local knowledge

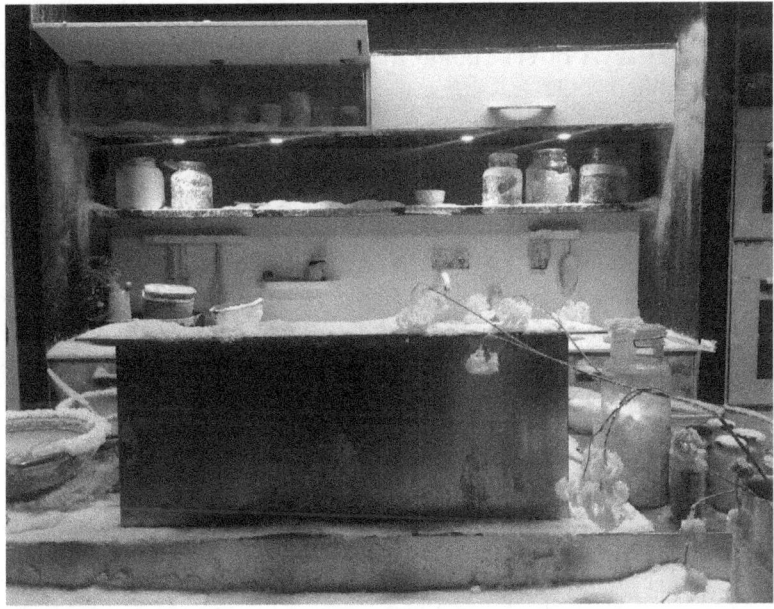

*Figure 2.2* Bianca Bondi, *The sacred spring and necessary reservoirs*, 2019 (detail), Lyon Biennale, 2019.

Photograph: Felicity Fenner.

and skills afforded "buy-in" from the people of Lyon, who make up three-quarters of the event's audience. Furthermore, this approach, together with the decision to restrict the geographical representation of artists in order to minimise international freight and travel, substantially reduced the carbon/ environmental footprint habitually imposed by biennales. In its commitment to environmental and local sustainability, the Fagor factory component of the 2019 Lyon Biennale demonstrated how even a major international biennale can reimagine its curatorial approach to respond in practical ways to global environmental and local economic issues, without compromising conceptual integrity.

The pandemic-induced pause of the early 2020s has since provided a timely opportunity for the resource-heavy biennale circuit to offer more than lip service to the ecological crisis. Before discussing in the next chapter two biennales with a stated mission to provide lasting environmental and cultural legacies, it is worth looking at recent editions of leading biennales in Ireland and Taiwan. Two very different exhibitions in very different parts of the world, the biennales of Taipei and Limerick have successfully created ecosystems within the gallery walls from artworks that respond to ecological crises both worldwide and local.

## 2020–2021 EVA International Biennial of Contemporary Art

Artists of today have largely rejected previous generations' philosophical interest in the sublime as they engage with the natural world as subject matter. Instead, they are taking a more grassroots perspective that is increasingly echoed in the curatorial strategies of the exhibitions in which their practice is featured. A good example is the 2020–2021 EVA International Biennial of Contemporary Art in Limerick, Ireland, which aimed to challenge historical perspectives of seeing the land as a resource to be tapped and exploited for profit through industrialised agriculture and global trade. With art projects exploring new ways of thinking through ideas of land and its contested values, the curatorial concept was based on the "Golden Vein" (more commonly referred to today as the "Golden Vale"), the 19th-century descriptor for the agriculturally rich Limerick region of Ireland.

Moving beyond a single museum or gallery to germinate in spaces across the city, the Biennial created a city-wide ecosystem, modest in its global outlook and grounded in its country of origin. Of special significance to Irish audiences, which due to travel restrictions imposed by the pandemic comprised the vast majority of visitors, was work by Irish artists made in response to local issues. The focus on ecological issues that visitors are cognisant of, if not directly impacted by, is a powerful vehicle of audience engagement with a high probability of raising awareness, investing a sense of urgency in individuals, and hopefully becoming a catalyst for expanding knowledge and concern for our natural environments.

Due to the pandemic, the single exhibition format of the scheduled 2020 EVA International Biennial was replaced with three smaller "phases" delivered over an 18-month period from September 2020 through to December 2021. Unlike other biennales and exhibitions around the world that quickly moved to an online-only presence when the pandemic forced galleries to close, the organisers of EVA International took a different approach. Though wanting to alleviate artist and audience health concerns around coming together for the traditionally more intensive exhibition model, they did not want to "go down the route of trying to translate exhibition experiences for a remote, online, audience".[13] Instead, the Biennial sought to build on society's increased empathy for others and for the environment that emerged as a silver lining to the pandemic, the curatorial team stating that they "also believe more than ever that art can play an important part in the way that society connects and re-connects itself".[14]

The main international "Guest Programme" featured over the three stages a relatively small-scale exhibition devised and overseen by Turkish curator Merve Elveren and was presented in six venues across Limerick. The first phase featured the work of just five artists, from Albania, England, Greece, and one from Ireland, Michele Horrigan. Horrigan's contribution was created in response to Limerick and the surrounding area, and as such was appropriately featured across a number of venues where it delivered a strong message about the long-term environmental ramifications of industry's imposition on and complex relationship with social and natural ecosystems.

For some years, Horrigan has been working on a project about the former island of Aughinish on the Shannon River estuary near Limerick in the west of Ireland, home to a nature reserve that includes Ireland's first butterfly sanctuary. Far from an environmental utopia, however, Aughinish is best known as the site of Europe's largest alumina refinery, which since the early 1980s has occupied almost the entire peninsula. Throughout the 1990s the refinery, which provides employment to a large proportion of the local population, was beset with environmental scandals: toxic deposits were found in the soil of nearby agricultural land, sulphur emissions posed a health threat, and the occurrence of livestock being born deformed was blamed on (though never proven to be caused by) the industrial process. As Horrigan summarises, "These concerns endure to highlight the struggle for survival between nature and industry, and between environment and economy."[15] Most alarmingly for many residents including the artist, a huge landfill site adjacent to the factory receives the toxic by-product of the refining process, known as "red mud", and continues to grow in size despite destroying natural ecosystems and rendering the surrounding land barren.

The centrepiece of Horrigan's project is titled *Stigma Damages*, a legal term used to describe a diminution in the value of property due to negative public perception or, increasingly, toxic contamination. It was presented at the Sailors Home, a former customs house now a cultural centre located at the entrance to Limerick Port, not far from the alumina plant. Through archival objects, documents, and videos that follow the journey of bauxite from mines in Africa and Brazil to its processing in Aughinish, Horrigan explored not only the devastation to the natural ecology of the land due to ongoing and unregulated industrialisation but also the impact of the factory's dominant presence on the adjacent town of Askeaton in County Limerick, the artist's childhood home.

Another component of Horrigan's project brought together seemingly random objects connected by aluminium, the end product of alumina. It included images of the mines and newspaper clippings reporting on toxic waste from

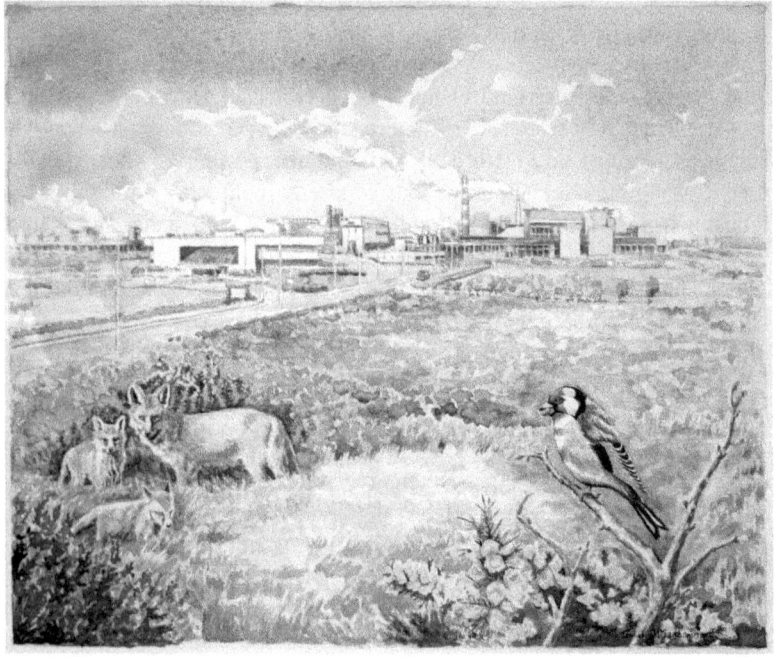

*Figure 2.3*  Michele Horrigan, *Stigma Damages*, 2011–ongoing (detail).
Source: Courtesy of the artist.

the Aughinish refinery, clothes and banknotes incorporating aluminium, and an illustrated history of the apex topping the Washington monument, made from aluminium which at the time of its fabrication in the 1880s was as rare and valuable as silver.[16] The artist's research revealed to exhibition visitors the role of their local alumina refinery in transforming a once precious metal into a material so accessible and ubiquitous that it has become a staple in every household. Rolls of kitchen foil and cans of cola were included in the display, everyday objects suggesting the complicity of society in facilitating damage to natural ecosystems, including valuable agricultural land such as the Golden Vein.

The concurrent "Platform Commissions" strand of the Biennial's first phase featured another four projects. Artists were selected from an open call, a new initiative designed to support artists based in Ireland. Like Horrigan's weaving together of personal and political threads, Eimear Walshe's *The Land Question: Where the fuck am I supposed to have sex?* is both a personal monologue on how land should be used and a form of political questioning as to how we have allowed land to be appropriated, economically and personally. A video installation activated by the viewer was described by one reviewer as a sermon-like monologue about contested land in the history of Ireland.[17]

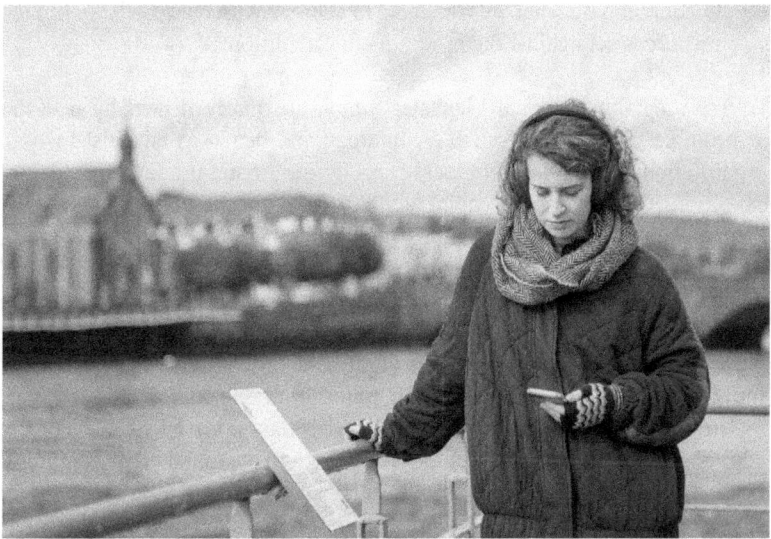

*Figure 2.4* Bora Baboci, *Predictions*, 2020, 39th EVA International, 2020.
Source: Courtesy of the artist and EVA International.
Photograph: Jed Niezgoda.

Also locally inspired was Albanian artist Bora Baboci's audio work, commissioned by the Biennial and created during an artist residency in Limerick. Activated by a QR code and downloaded onto a smartphone, users listen to a fictive weather forecast describing the River Shannon running dry and the bureaucratic response: "A small desert like land has been forming on the river. . . . The city is considering new zoning procedures. . . . There is speculation on the first property claims."[18] Meshing fact and fiction, the work predicts the dire consequences of climate change for the river, one of Ireland's key waterways.

Coincidentally, the Biennial had abandoned the mega-exhibition model in late 2018, implementing a new exhibition format in a bid to ensure future sustainability and capacity. Given the global health crisis with its resultant stay-at-home orders and closure of international borders, visitation and media coverage of the Biennial was inevitably diminished in comparison to previous years and to those 2020 biennials less affected by the pandemic such as Sydney's (see Chapter 3). Biennial director Matt Packer was realistic:

> Our audience and press impact were much more reduced than with previous editions of the biennial, but we anticipated this. Given the gravity of the crisis, we didn't allow ourselves to feel disappointed. I'm very encouraged by what we were able to achieve with our relatively limited resources set against the most adverse conditions.[19]

Unlike most international biennales which are partly driven by a desire to promote cultural tourism, EVA International began as an artist-focused organisation seeking to build local capacity for artistic production and consumption. The Limerick Biennial of 2020–2021 is a useful exemplar of how biennales can be envisaged at this time when nature seems to be turning against humankind. Rather than reflecting and ruminating on the ecological crisis, the exhibition proactively engaged with local audiences by focusing on the big issues that play out in close-to-home scenarios. Furthermore, the phased delivery adopted in response to the pandemic provides a useful model for biennales seeking to achieve momentum from one edition to the next.

The recurrent international exhibition that has a proven track record in adopting this accumulative curatorial approach to the land and its communities, on a much larger and ambitious scale, is the Echigo-Tsumari Art Triennale discussed in Chapter 3. Other more traditionally conceived biennales, however, have in recent exhibitions demonstrated a sustained commitment to thematic directions across editions, in order to establish generative legacies including environmental outcomes. The continuum of subject matter addressed from the 2018 to 2020 editions of the Taipei Biennial, for example, represents a distinct shift in the organisation's curatorial approach. Specifically, the 2020 exhibition took advantage of thematic traction achieved by the previous one, bringing its own curatorial stamp to the exhibition but also eschewing the more typical curatorial approach to biennales of renewal and reinvention.

## 2018 and 2020 Taipei Biennial

Both the 2018 and 2020 editions of the Taipei Biennial addressed environmental issues, including with ongoing projects involving human interactions with the natural environment. While not an unexpected subject matter given the island's natural beauty and prevalence in Taiwanese culture of its natural environments, the continuity of theme from one edition to the next suggested a rejection of usual biennale curatorial approaches that preference renewal over reiteration. While the 2018 Biennial conceived of the museum as an interconnected ecosystem, the 2020 edition unpacked the deep divisions between, for example, Donald Trump and Greta Thunberg, through artworks that sought to unite humanity's approach to climate change.

Like the 2019 Lyon Biennale, the Taipei Biennials were firmly grounded in the place in which they are staged, while also responding to global issues. Historically, Taiwanese people have an inherent understanding and rapport with the natural world. Taiwan's original inhabitants, known as Yuanzhumin, are of Malayo-Polynesian heritage and have lived in Taiwan for at least 10,000 or perhaps 20,000 years and, despite ongoing claims for self-government, retain a distinct identity as the Taiwanese First Nation ("Aboriginal") people. Since the 17th century, the island's culture has been shaped by settlers of Han Chinese heritage, who now make up around 80 percent of the population, and in modern times by Western nations and Japan, who occupied Taiwan for the first half of the 20th century. As part of the country's ongoing attempt to forge an identity independent of mainland China, the 1980s witnessed a drive by the government of Taiwan to advance arts and culture ahead of the lifting of martial law in 1987: in 1982 a National Arts Academy was established, and in 1983 the Taipei Fine Arts Museum (TFAM) opened, the island's first modern art museum and home of the Taipei Biennial.

TFAM established the Taipei Biennial in 1996, a year after establishing the Taiwan pavilion at the Venice Biennale as a way of distinguishing the country's art practice from that of China's. The Taipei Biennial was one of a raft of biennials instigated in the 1990s including in Asia following the launch in 1993 of the first Asia-Pacific Triennial of Contemporary Art at the Queensland Art Gallery in Brisbane, Australia. The Gwangju Biennale in South Korea (since 1995) and Shanghai Biennale in China (1996) are just two of the other continuing international biennials in Asia begun at the same time.

While it started as an open-entry event primarily restricted to the immediate geographic region, the 2010 Taipei Biennial exhibition was predicated on a re-thinking and re-setting of the Biennial. Prior to 2010 the Biennial was directed by a pair of curators, before switching to a single (Western) curator until 2018, after which the dual model of a high-profile international and Taiwanese arts professional was reintroduced. During the single-curator period, German curator Anselm Franke oversaw the 2012 edition and French curator Nicolas Bourriaud the 2014 edition. Whether the shifting curatorial models were part of a longer-term strategy to articulate a Taiwanese cultural identity or to absorb the Biennial into a more generic international biennale culture by diluting its cultural specificity is a moot point.[20] Nevertheless, whatever the political motivation in terms of international recognition, it was the appointment of Bourriaud that signalled the Biennial's continuing thematic preference for an environmental focus.

Bourriaud's exhibition took *The Great Acceleration* as its title with the Anthropocene as its subject, proposing that

> the more real the collective impact of the species is, the less contemporary individuals feel capable of influencing their surrounding reality [leading to] the emergence an unprecedented political coalition between the individual/citizen and a new subordinate class: animals, vegetation, minerals and the atmosphere, all imperilled by a techno-industrial system now clearly detached from civil society.[21]

Embracing this new philosophical conundrum as the exhibition's starting point, Bourriaud collated and commissioned an unabashedly Eurocentric exhibition with a handful of works from Brazil and just eight from the host country of Taiwan. The overwhelming majority of artists were from the traditional art centres of New York, London, Paris, and Berlin, a monocultural base that compromised the scope of the exhibition's conceptual ambition.

TFAM Senior Curator Jo Hsiao made a case for Bourriaud's global view by suggesting that the curatorial concept was in part inspired by traditional Chinese Daoist thought and that the exhibition successfully reinterpreted both Western and Eastern cosmological views of the world.[22] Despite many individual works that proposed cross-species relationships and futuristic interdependencies between animate and inanimate forces and human and non-human beings, the exhibition in its entirety was one of reflection rather than stimulation: it failed to break away from traditional Western curatorial traditions of displaying artworks in an archaeological sequence within the museum walls. Eastern notions of non-linear time and the universe being underpinned by spiritual connection were largely not evident.

The exception and most memorable work was *My Teacher Tortoise* by Japanese-born, Berlin-based artist Shimabuku. An iterative project originally created in 2011 for a solo exhibition in London, it features a large, live tortoise alone in a stark white pen.[23] At the Taipei Biennial a framed sign on the adjacent wall read "Stop, Stop and Think, Return, Occasionally Run", inviting viewers to take a leaf out of the tortoise's life and approach life in a slow, meditative and meaningful way. The artist is well known for his understated humour and deliberations on human behaviour. Perhaps funny when first encountered, the most engaging qualities of this work were the invitation to "people watch" – to observe other people encountering and pondering the tortoise – and the imagined insight into the mindset of another being, one that has some important lessons for humans perpetually on the treadmill of "the great acceleration". As such, *My Teacher Tortoise* was also one of the few works to incorporate Eastern thought in a way that was meaningful also to Western audiences. This very succinct intersection of different value systems, however, also gave rise to cultural misunderstanding: some Western audiences were concerned for the wellbeing of the tortoise, whose enclosure was devoid of any comfort or amenity, let alone plants or food. In one instance, concerns were raised with museum staff and the following day the tortoise had been removed. A public relations disaster was averted with a sign explaining that "The teacher tortoise is off for a sun spa!"[24]

Bourriaud's 2014 Taipei Biennial was thoughtful and reflective, as would be expected from a philosopher-curator, but later editions of the Biennial more convincingly represented the global shift towards a reassessment of the role of art and exhibitions in a time of ecological crisis. The 2016 edition, curated by Corinne Diserens, continued Bourriaud's essentially philosophical approach to art's potential as a provocateur for new possibilities with an exploration, in the curator's words, of "different practices of thought, the invention of discursive and performative apparatuses, and the production of models and images leading to heterogeneous narrations allowing transdisciplinary artistic experiences".[25]

The 2018 and 2020 editions, in contrast, offered more urgent and pragmatic responses to current issues and are therefore of more interest here. Both editions initiated collaborative projects with local communities interested in addressing environmental issues. With half the number of artists than the 2016 Biennial and a third less than Bourriaud's exhibition, the 2018 exhibition encouraged substantial, ambitious projects, many of them interdisciplinary in nature. Helen Mayer Harrison and Newton Harrison's *Making Earth* installation (1970/2018), for example, was a centrepiece of the 2018 Biennial both physically and thematically. Pioneers of the American eco art movement, the Harrisons' original impetus for creating the work was their recognition that topsoil was endangered in many parts of the world by industry and development, and that artists could through eco art interventions reveal to people the importance of nutritious soil in maintaining healthy ecosystems. Following their earliest collaborations, they have in the ensuing five decades worked with biologists, ecologists, architects, and planners to support biodiversity by multidisciplinary solutions to environmental challenges, often involving other artists and local communities. Their working methodology was echoed in the curatorial approach to the 2018 Taipei Biennial.

Titled *Post-Nature: A Museum as an Ecosystem* and co-curated by veteran socially engaged Taiwanese artist Mali Wu and British curator Francesco Manacorda (curator of *Radical Nature* in 2009 – see Chapter 1), the exhibition set out to examine the ever-changing qualities of natural ecosystems while also creating an ecosystem within the gallery itself. Its curatorial innovation lay in the move from a display of discrete objects and installations to a network of conceptually and thematically interconnected projects, many of them unfolding over the course of the exhibition both inside the walls of TFAM and off-site. In some ways the exhibition continued Bourriaud's preoccupation with post-human relationships, working with a similar theme to put into action the possibilities offered by artistic practice to navigate and survive a rapidly changing natural ecology.

Unlike previous dual-curator editions of the Biennial, the partnership between Wu and Manacorda rigorously supported the ecological sustainable aims of their 2018 exhibition. Previous curatorial partnerships had been fraught with tension between global and local concerns, compared by one critic to "inviting an international superstar to perform with a local band".[26] The challenges of articulating a cultural identity are unusually exacerbated in relation to the Taipei Biennial, given the complexity of Taiwan's political relationship with China. The high standing of Mali Wu in Taipei as an artist, cultural leader and educator, however, ensured meaningful participation from Taiwanese artists and artist collectives.

In their introduction to the exhibition, the curators acknowledged the need for change and declared their trust in artists to proffer solutions to ecological crises:

> Since the beginning of time, politics and economics have been concerned with forward progression and human survival; this is now beginning to evolve into a search for new and experimental plans for sustainability, enabling the survival of both human and non-human beings. Projecting into the post-human world, artists are specially positioned to imagine and invent methods by which we can maintain

biodiversity and strengthen the fragile interdependence among living organisms.[27]

Ironically, it was a major installation that was commissioned for but physically removed from other works in the Biennial that provided continuity between Bourriaud's theme in 2014 and the concept of a museum as an ecosystem in 2018. The Brazilian art collective Opavivará! designed a characteristically Bourriaud-like relational space in the expansive lobby area of the museum, inviting visitors to slow down, socialise, and take a few minutes rest before venturing into the exhibition. An octagonal structure supporting 16 hammocks and activated by traditional Brazilian tea ceremonies, *Formosa Decelarator* was referred to by the artists as a "temple of idleness, an invitation to inactivity, a space that worships the non-productive and non-active".[28] Offering an alternative narrative to the 2014 Biennial's commentary on the inevitable outcome for all species of the Anthropocene's race to destruction, the opportunity for a physical and mental recalibration provided clarifying pause for reflection and connection. Four years later, the 2018 curators referred to Bourriaud's theme in noting that environmental challenges "have accelerated, exponentially increasing the risk of overall destruction" yet, in a sign of changing curatorial imperatives in response to ecological crises, shifted the exhibition's raison d'être from one of rumination to activation.[29]

Wu and Manacorda's 2018 Biennial was interdisciplinary (it included documentary film, science, literature, architecture and urban planning) and generated new knowledge through workshops and research forums. With over 30 percent of participants coming from non-art backgrounds and disciplines, it aimed to reframe the role of the biennale as a participant in rather than observer of social change. They envisaged TFAM as "a discursive space for collaboration, transformation, cooperation, diffusion and absorption", reimagining the museum as "as a social actor, which can become integrated in its local community and culture".[30] Self-reflexive, relational, and sometimes didactic artworks took the form of oyster mushroom farming (Tue Greenfort, Denmark), a workshop for asthma sufferers using air harvested from Taipei city (Ting-Tong Chang, Taiwan) and another teaching participants about the positive properties of weed species (Zo Lin, Taiwan), a programme of lectures by civil rights and animal rights organisations on the subjects of dehumanisation, oppression, and the abuse of nature (Gustafsson and Haapoja, Finland), and an architect-designed visualisation of live climate data from inside the museum (Huai-Wen Chang, Taiwan).

The exhibition also included collections of documentary material from environmental artist teams such as Futurefarmers (USA), the Taiwan Thousand Miles Trail Association, and the Open Green project, which

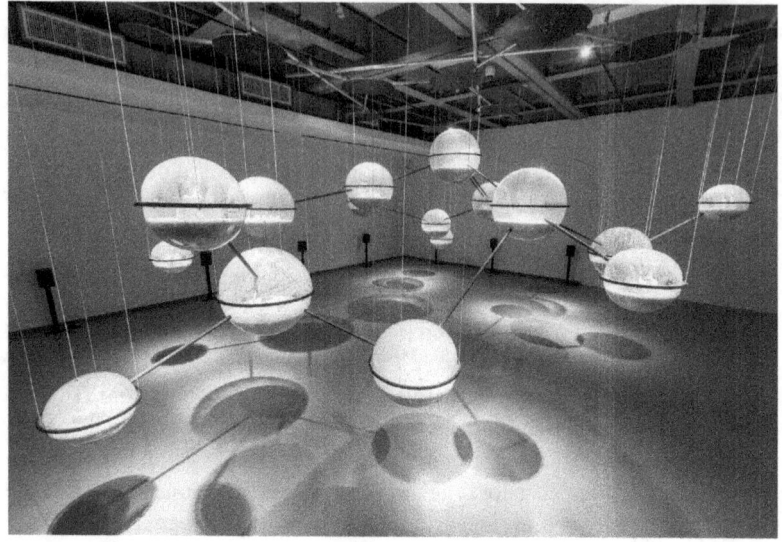

*Figure 2.5* Mycelium Network Society, Taipei Biennial, 2018.
Source: Courtesy of the artists and TFAM.

encourages Taipei's residents, schools, and other community groups to transform through greening underutilised urban and suburban spaces, echoing Fritz Haeg's *Edible Estates* though including also the establishment of new spaces for passive recreation. Although essentially didactic in content and presentation, the inclusion of such projects in biennales, while not necessarily contributing to the visual impact of the exhibition, does reveal how artworks themselves, in addition to associated public programmes, can influence environmental activism and inspire behaviour change. As one article observed, the exhibition was "a valuable searchlight into the social and political relevance of global biennials, as well as their contention for legitimacy and significance as agents of social transformation".[31]

One of the major installations in the 2018 Biennial comprised a living network of mycelium colonies by the Mycelium Network Society, a team of artists from Europe and Taiwan. They installed a series of suspended glass aquariums containing fungus and spores, a functioning model of a mycelium network that illustrates how a museum can host a living ecosystem. Symbolically, the mycelium network connected natural ecosystems across national borders to nodes in France, the United Kingdom, the United States, and Taiwan. Through a series of electronic sensors, transmitters, and receivers, changes within the living mycelium were transmitted between the pods, "conjuring an imaginary techno-organic network".[32] Experienced within the white cube of the gallery, the work conveyed the sense of a natural ecosystem, albeit resembling alien worlds enclosed in plastic pods as if part of a global scientific experiment.

Like many artist-led projects informed by science and driven by a desire to foster greater appreciation of the natural world and its precious ecosystems, it was the kind of project that some may argue is not "art" while others might applaud its capacity to transcend such pigeon-holing, which in the context of addressing climate change is in any case meaningless: the point is not whether it constitutes art, agriculture, or science, but whether it effectively conveys new knowledge. In this case it did, but the lack of aesthetic appeal, beyond the installation resembling a cross between a scientific laboratory and a museum model of planets, illustrates the conundrum faced by artists and curators feeling increasingly compelled to address the ever more urgent ecological crisis. The inclusion of objects or ideas that would not normally be classified as "art" is a strategy that as noted earlier, dates back to Harald Szeemann's 1972 documenta 5, which presented "an elaborate exhibitionary structure populated both by art and non-art objects".[33]

The work elicited a similar response to that of the *Freize* critic writing about Manacorda's *Radical Nature* a decade earlier, in that it "could be mistaken for the research and development wing of some insane urban scientist".[34] If art is to be brought into the service of public messaging about climate change – its primary impetus being the visual interpretation of scientific information and the proposition of creative environmental solutions – does it risk compromising audience engagement?

In his catalogue essay for *Radical Nature*, T.J. Demos cited Bruno Latour's questioning back in 2004 of the status of art that had become "flattened" by artists' uncritical acceptance of humans' capacity to effect change. As Demos explains:

> If artists and cultural practitioners refuse to surrender their discerning consideration of scientific dictates, then what do they do, as French philosopher Bruno Latour asks, when their methodological commitment to resisting the self-evidence of 'truth' prevents them from accepting the truth of impending ecological crisis, which potentially allies them with climate-change sceptics?[35]

In the light of this consideration some 15 years before he was appointed as curator of the Taipei Biennial, it is interesting to reflect on how Latour approached the task of curating an exhibition dedicated to addressing the current ecological crises and staged at the height of a global health pandemic. The Biennial embodied Latour's perspective on the connection between ecological crises on Earth and current-day space exploration by billionaires, exemplified in his 2018 book *Down to Earth*, on which the 2020 Berlin exhibition discussed in the Introduction Chapter 1 was premised:

> [T]he conviction, shared by some powerful people, that the ecological threat is real and that the only way for them to survive is to abandon any pretence at sharing a common future with the rest of the world. Hence their flight offshore and their massive investment in climate change denial.[36]

The 2020 Taipei Biennial was led by Latour and developed in collaboration with a small team of three, comprising curator Martin Guinard and Taiwanese cultural producer Eva Lin. As one of very few international biennales to proceed as planned in 2020 due to the global spread of the COVID-19 virus, the event was appropriately responsive to the exigent crises facing the world at that critical moment in time. Set very specifically against the backdrop of the worsening ecological and related pandemic crises, and the apparent impossibility among global leaders to agree on solutions, their aim was to diffuse geopolitical tensions over the way forward by presenting and comparing a diversity of views. They used the concept of different planets to present the responses by artists to the conflicting ideological and policy positions, creating a fictional planetarium inside the museum where artists, activists, and scientists explored differing views of the world.

The "planets" were arranged thematically as Globalisation, Security, Escape, Alternate Gravity, and Terrestrial. Building on the multidisciplinary aspects of the 2018 Biennial, the 2020 exhibition team proactively collaborated with scholars from a number of disciplines to explore intersections between human and non-human worlds, the planets conceived as a speculative "series of thought experiments".[37] Specialists interested in scientific controversies from different fields were invited to participate. They included pollution experts, urban planners, geologists, and chemists, to work with artists to explore what Latour refers to as "the whole ecological mutation", deploying the metaphor of planets as "a very powerful way to dramatize the main issue of politics of ecology of the present moment in the 21st century".[38]

The creation of a planetary ecosystem within the ecosystem of the museum itself was an apt metaphor for the discrete yet inevitably interconnected "bubbles" that humans inhabit, as has been starkly revealed by the rolling waves of ideological currents away from centrist politics in recent years, from Trump and Brexit to the ascendance of the Taliban and China. The colossal realignment of international power relations being brazenly pursued by Xi Jingping's autocratic government poses a material threat to Taiwan's sense of self-determination. Already, due to its lack of recognition as an independent state, Taiwan has an ambivalent relationship both with nations of the Northern Hemisphere in which it is geographically located and with the Global South, the loose collection of developing countries in Asia, Africa, the Middle East, and Pacific to which it technically does not belong. Coincidentally, the exhibition at TFAM immediately prior to the 2020 Biennial explored this complex relationship, acknowledging that the "South" represents a specific yet constantly changing imagination more closely linked to value systems than geographic locations.[39] In geopolitical terms, therefore, Taiwan can be characterised as being in a "bubble" of its own.

When the 2020 Biennial was first announced, Latour directly referenced Swedish teenage climate crusader Greta Thunberg and former US President Trump as representing the two opposing poles of the world's ideological approach to the ecological crisis.[40] Indeed, these two protagonists in the climate debate during Trump's presidency – who for many represented straightforward manifestations of good and evil – are distinctly appositional on their perception of planetary worth. When president, Trump directed resources at a programme to expedite an increased human presence in outer space, albeit demonstrating a lack of planetary knowledge when doing so, declaring that Mars was part of the Moon.[41] (It was a missed opportunity by NASA to offer a private, auto-piloted presidential rocket, guaranteed to stay in orbit until Mars was located on the Moon.)

In Latour and Guinard's exhibition, the rationale underpinning Elon Musk's pursuit of colonising Mars and the US Government's Moon programme was captured in "Planet Escape", which was based on the understanding that "none of these are solutions that can be shared with the billions of people left behind".[42] Unless immediate action is taken as urged in the Intergovernmental Panel on Climate Change (IPCC) report published in 2021, most of us will be faced with the worst consequences of the current ecological crisis, a fact confronted by works situated in other "planets" (sections) of the exhibition, most specifically in the "Planet Terrestrial" group of works which reassessed the state of Earth – the land and its water, soil, plants, rocks, and fauna.[43] Taiwanese artist Yung-Ta Chang, for example, undertook dual residencies at scientific observatories in Potsdam, Germany, and the Taroko Gorge in the centre of Taiwan, exploring "Critical Zones" where geographic extremes such as earthquakes and landslides are active. The resulting installation presented rocks and fauna in tall glass vials, deploying the visual lexicon of scientific instruments to convey the artist's impressions of these precariously balanced spaces at the coalface of climate change.

The first planet of the fictional planetarium was "Planet Globalization", which is formed as a "result of international exchange and trade since the 1980s", based on "promises of development and economic growth in complete denial of planetary limitations".[44] The section contained works reflecting on different kinds of connectivity, such as that between artistic practice and international law in the case of a major installation by French artist Frank Leibovici and former criminal law analyst Julien Seroussi in which visitors were invited to interact with the work by reconfiguring shards of "evidence" to create alternative narratives. The insinuation of the work's inclusion is that scientific evidence of climate change can be manipulated by individuals and leaders to suit their beliefs or political ambitions. A key work illustrating the ecological interconnection was by Taiwanese artist Aruwai Kaumakan, a welcome prominence that was in contrast to previous editions of the Biennial in which the most high-profile works tended to be by well-known foreign artists. A textile artist recently and permanently displaced from her village by a destructive climatic catastrophe, Kaumakan was commissioned by the Biennial to create a woven installation *Vines in the Mountains* (2020). Using Lemikalic, a traditional Paiwan technique of weaving in concentric circles, Kaumakan co-opted assistance from other villagers, all of whom had lost their homes in the disaster. With tendrils reaching from woven circular hubs, which in relation to the Biennial's curatorial ecosystem could be read as planets, the work sought to forge a reconnection to place through collaboration with others similarly displaced.

More directly responsive to the environmental debate was an installation by MILLIØNS (American designers Zeina Koreitem and John May) which investigated the historic ecological destruction and long-term planetary impact of urban construction, taking as its case study Mies van der Rohe's icon of modern architecture, the Seagram Building in Manhattan. *The Ghost Acres of Architecture* (2020) provided documentation of the building's carbon footprint beginning with the extraction of raw materials in different parts of the world in the 1950s. Through data visualisation and projections, the research proposed that even just one city skyscraper has a harmful territorial reach and that architects need to be accountable not only for the environmental design integrity of the finished structure but from the moment of its conception before materials are sourced and construction commences.

The application to a real-life example that dates back almost three generations makes this an especially persuasive, thought-provoking, and, given the design background of its authors, refreshingly self-critical analysis of the building profession's contribution to ecological crises. How audiences are expected to respond to this information, particularly those working in the fields of design and construction, is less clear. What the exhibition did succeed in conveying is that, despite feeling that the "bubbles" we inhabit are separate planets, the world is intrinsically interconnected, especially in this age of globalisation.

In an interview with Artnet's Naomi Rae, curators Latour and Guinard acknowledged the irony of deploying the forum of an international art biennale, with its inevitable carbon footprint, to sound the alarm on climate change.[45] To reduce the exhibition's adverse environmental impacts, they recycled display walls and where possible reproduced works on site rather than fly them in from (mostly) Europe and the United States. A blow for visitation levels but a boost to their carbon-reduction crusade was the unforeseen arrival of a global pandemic. Since 2010 the Taipei Biennial has become a fixture on the itinerary of international biennale art jetsetters: in 2020 the audience was drawn almost entirely from within Taiwan, unexpectedly re-focusing the exhibition's engagement strategies to meet the concerns not of an informed or market-oriented international art audience but of a diverse general public curious to find relevance locally in the issues being addressed. Even the concept of different planets, for example, took on a new significance when applied exclusively to local audiences. The inference of metaphorical planets being aligned with certain cultures or countries lost impact with the closure of international borders. Instead, the analogy of planets invited deeper consideration of how different educational backgrounds, religious beliefs, and political leanings can in turn lead to a range of viewpoints on the shared climate crisis within a relatively small city of 2.6 million people.

As discussed in the Introduction, this shift in the audience base contributed to a reframing of the values inherent to cultural capital. These new types of audience engagement were fully explored in Eva Lin's suite of public programmes devised for the Biennial, which aimed to "spark an epiphany that prompts people to adopt a new perspective, and perhaps even go as far as to change their minds about how they approach nature, ecology, globalization, and more".[46] A diverse and accessible schedule of talks, workshops, and participatory programmes served to activate the more cerebral aims of the exhibition, bringing to life its core ideas and proposals with novel activities targeted at a range of audiences.

A decade earlier, public programmes accompanying international biennales were devised and tacked on by the host institution, following a similar format to visitor programmes for any major exhibition. Guided tours by staff and volunteers, expert addresses and panel discussions, and a few artist and curator talks during the opening week were until recently the standard fare. Like public art that is plonked as an afterthought onto a site rather than integrated during the early stages of urban design, public programmes conceived in isolation from an exhibition's curatorial planning stages can be perceived as secondary rather than core to the overarching concept. In the case of the Sydney (see Chapter 3) and Taipei biennales in 2020, the public programmes were not plonk programmes following a museological format but devised by the curatorial team as central to the biennale experience, ensuring they were not only relevant but contributed as agents of change.

Like the exhibition itself, in which different "planets" provided an inventive lens through which to discuss hackneyed debates around environmental politics, the public programmes of the 2020 Taipei Biennial made participants aware through fun and inventive actions of the many obstacles faced by different stakeholders dealing with ecological crises. Foremost was the "Theater of Negotiations", which invited tertiary students from various universities to participate in debates on the ecological crisis, including issues directly affecting Taiwan such as food security and renewable energies. The debaters were mentored by researchers from the Science, Technology and Society Association, a leading academic think tank in Taiwan focused on interdisciplinary integrated thinking, and by the Center for Democratic Innovation and Governance, aimed at building capacity for mutual understanding, negotiation, and empowerment to influence public policy. The students assumed the roles of diverse stakeholders, such as lobbyists, lawyers,

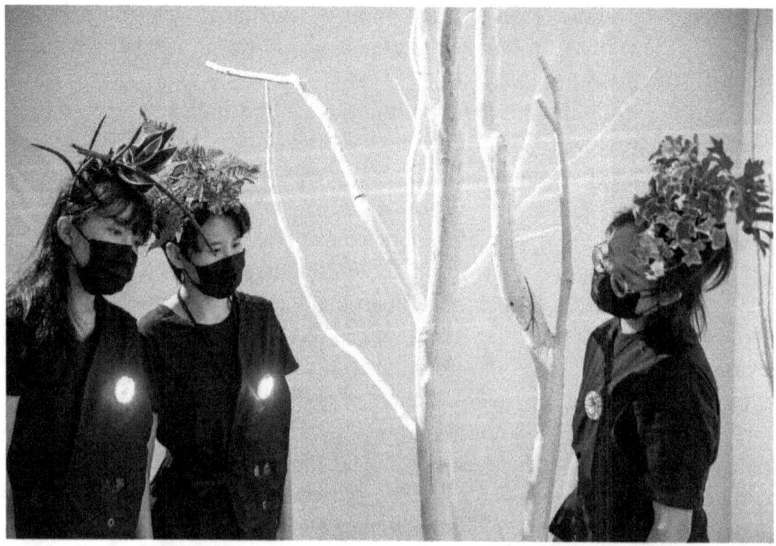

*Figure 2.6* "Saunter in the Air", Public Programme, Taipei Biennial, 2020.
Source: Courtesy of TFAM.

politicians, and local residents, learning to be open to others' views while persuasively presenting their case.

Another public programme, whimsically titled "Saunter in the Air", adapted the Situationists' "dérive" practice of discovering little-known and hidden aspects of the city by walking aimlessly without purpose nor the aid of maps. In the Biennial version, participants were provided with an air-pollution sensor to wear around the streets of Taipei. It was aimed at raising awareness of levels of air pollution, allowing participants to measure and compare air quality. For another, "Arts of Coming Down to Earth", environmental engineer Stéphane Verlet-Bottéro was commissioned to calculate the exhibition's $CO_2$ emissions, a self-assessment project not dissimilar to others being conducted by exhibition organisers, including those by Australian artist Lucas Ihlein for the MCA and Biennale of Sydney.[47] At the Taipei Biennial the initiative included a symposium and workshop, maximising the potential to analyse the exhibition's carbon footprint and with a longer-term ambition to effect behaviour change by TFAM and other museums and arts organisations hosting large international exhibitions.

The 2020 Taipei Biennial programmes were an integral part of the conceptual premise of the exhibition, devised from the earliest stages of planning in close collaboration with Latour and Guinard. Like the exhibition itself, they were developed in response to prevailing environmental challenges, and their shape further moulded by rapidly evolving world events. Of particular influence was Greta Thunberg's powerful retort to Trump in her speech at the World Economic Forum in Davos (the manifestation of an archetypal meeting between different "planets") and the unfolding pandemic that revealed the deadly power of nature to reject human incursions into its precious ecosystems.

Lin's public programmes built on audiences' newly sharpened understanding of global connectivity, the lessons of working together in pursuit of common gains during 2020s unrelenting periods of disease contagion and lockdown successfully applied by Lin to the Biennial setting. The planned public programmes for the 2020 Biennale of Sydney were similarly aimed at actively engaging exhibition visitors as participants in activities crafted to reveal new understandings and insights into the world. Many were to be led by First Nations keepers of traditional knowledges regarding natural environments: had they not been quashed by the sudden imposition of health restrictions, the programmes in Sydney would have also offered new avenues for mutual learning and enriched appreciation of alternative perspectives.

The 2019–2021 biennales discussed here in Lyon, Limerick, and Taipei articulate strategies for engaging audiences in ways that are likely to affect knowledge transfer and even behaviour change in response to the ecological crisis: exhibitions conceived as ecosystems of interrelated works, public programmes that are accessible and participatory, and art projects of relevance to the communities in which the biennales are staged. In each of these exhibitions the curators have approached the biennale as a vehicle of public engagement with the issues of our times, laying the foundations for the conversations to continue beyond their biennale and into the next edition.

Most significantly, between the 2018 and 2020 editions of the Taipei Biennial, there was a clear continuation of core themes around ecological crises, scientific inquiry, and environmental activism. For the incoming 2020 curatorial team led by Bruno Latour, the willingness not only to acknowledge but to extend on the subject matter embraced by Manacorda and Wu revealed the shared sense of urgency across the two editions. Latour's curatorial approach validated the importance of the 2018 edition while simultaneously empowering his own. The Biennale of Sydney is similarly mapping key directions across editions, as discussed in the following chapter.

## Notes

1  Augusta Pownall, "We Don't Have the Power to Stop Our Extinction", *Dezeen*, 22 February, 2019, www.dezeen.com/2019/02/22/paola-antonelli-extinction-milan-triennale-broken-nature-exhibition/ (accessed 12 June 2019).
2  Preview, "Manif d'art 9, 2019", https://universes.art/en/manifdart/2019 (accessed 1 July 2021).
3  Greta Thunberg, "Our House Is on Fire", Speech 25 January, 2019. Published as " 'Our House is on Fire': Greta Thunberg, 16, Urges Leaders to Act on Climate", *The Guardian*, 26 January, 2019, www.theguardian.com/environment/2019/jan/25/our-house-is-on-fire-greta-thunberg16-urges-leaders-to-act-on-climate (accessed 1 July 2021).
4  According to the Biennial Foundation prior to Raspail's departure, "Since the Lyon Biennale's inception in 1991, its artistic director Thierry Raspail has always suggested a key word to his guest curators. . . . for each edition the artistic director builds the event's identity, choosing a curator or curatorial team to devise an artistic project in close collaboration", www.biennialfoundation.org/biennials/lyon-biennale/ (accessed 2 June 2021).
5  Jean de Loisy's co-curators were Daria de Beauvais, Adélaïde Blanc, Yoann Gourmel, Matthieu Lilièvre, Vittora Matarrese, Claire Moulène and Hugo Vitrani.
6  Isabelle Bertolotti, Exhibition Guide, *When Water Comes Together with Other Water: 15th Lyon Biennale of Contemporary Art*, Lyon, Fage éditions, 2019, p. 138.
7  Margaret Carrigan, " 'Post-Industrial' Biennale de Lyon to Examine Shifting Social and Economic Experience of the Region", *The Art Newspaper*, 11 September, 2019, www.theartnewspaper.com/preview/manufacturing-the-lyon-biennial (accessed 6 June 2021).
8  Yoann Gourmel et al., Exhibition Guide, *When Water Comes Together with Other Water: 15th Lyon Biennale of Contemporary Art*, p. 150.
9  Gourmel et al., Exhibition Guide, *When Water Comes Together with Other Water*, p. 150.

10 Gourmel et al., Exhibition Guide, *When Water Comes Together with Other Water*, p. 213.
11 Bianca Bondi wall label text, Lyon Biennale.
12 Gourmel et al., Exhibition Guide, *When Water Comes Together with Other Water*, p. 150.
13 Christian Oxenius, "Interview with Matt Packer, Director and CEO of EVA International in Biennials in Times of COVID-19", *International Biennial Association*, 6 November, 2020, https://biennialassociation.org/biennials-in-times-of-COVID19-eva-international/ (accessed 29 June 2021).
14 Matt Packer, "Introduction, Phase 1 Programme", *2021 EVA International*, www.eva.ie/wp-content/uploads/2020/09/EVA_Phase_1_Programme_WEB-Version.pdf (accessed 27 June 2021).
15 Michele Horrigan, "Stigma Damages", https://michelehorrigan.com/app/uploads/2014/07/Stigma_Damages.pdf (accessed 27 June 2021).
16 www.nps.gov/wamo/index.htm (accessed 29 June 2021).
17 Theo Hynan-Ratcliffe, "EVA International Phase 1: The Eye, The Voice", *Visual Artists Ireland*, https://visualartistsireland.com/eva-international-phase-1-the-eye-the-voice?fbclid=IwAR2MMvIPan3h7eW2CZ8jxva20rnTtZy18hgH33M5GvN4ndyVf9Gpx4gEShk (accessed 29 June 2021).
18 Excerpt from the audio of *Predictions*, 2020, www.eva.ie/bora-baboci-predictions-2020/
19 Oxenius, "Interview with Matt Packer".
20 Pei-Yi Lu, "Why Don't We Sing? Rethinking the Curatorial Mechanisms of the Taipei Biennial for the First Twenty Years (1996–2016)", *The Korean Society of Art Theories*, December, 2017, vol. 24, pp. 104–126.
21 Nicolas Bourriaud, "The Politics of the Anthropocene: Humanity, Things and Reification in Contemporary Art", *Taipei Biennial 2014: The Great Acceleration*, Taipei, Taipei Fine Arts Museum, 2014, p. 10.
22 Jo Hsiao, "The Circuit Chart of the Great Acceleration", in *Taipei Biennial 2014: The Great Acceleration*, p. 72.
23 Wilkinson Gallery, London, 6 May – 5 June, 2011.
24 The author and her curatorial students from UNSW Sydney enquired to TFAM staff about the tortoise's wellbeing, 9–10 November 2014. No response was received, and the following day the tortoise had been removed from the display. It is entirely possible, of course, that this was in fact the creature's scheduled day off and that the students' concern played no role in its temporary disappearance.
25 The 2016 Taipei Biennial announcement on e-flux by the Taipei Fine Arts Museum, 7 July, 2016, www.e-flux.com/announcements/52417/taipei-biennial-2016gestures-and-archives-of-the-present-genealogies-of-the-future/ (accessed 10 August 2021).
26 Huei-Hwa Cheng, "How Can We Face the Reality? The Declaration of Absence in the Taipei Biennial Opening", in Lu, "Why Don't We Sing?" p. 113.
27 Francesco Manacorda and Mali Wu, "Post-Nature – A Museum as an Ecosystem: Curatorial Statement by Mali Wu and Francesco Mancorda", *Universes in Universe*, https://universes.art/en/taipei-biennial/2018/curatorial-text (accessed 10 August 2021).
28 Exhibition guide, *The Great Acceleration*, Taipei, Taipei Fine Arts Museum, 2014.

29  Manacorda and Wu, "Curatorial Statement".
30  Manacorda and Wu, "Curatorial Statement".
31  Jenifer Chao and Panos Kompatsiaris, "Curating Climate Change: The Taipei Biennial as an Environmental Problem Solver", *Journal of Contemporary Chinese Art*, vol. 7, no. 1, pp. 7–26, https://doi.org/10.1386/jcca_00017_1 (accessed 13 August 2021).
32  Francesco Manacorda and Mali Wu (eds.), Exhibition Guide, *Post-Nature – A Museum as an Ecosystem*, Taipei, Taipei Museum of Fine Arts, p. 39.
33  Bruce Altshuler, "Introduction", in *Biennials and Beyond – Exhibitions That Made Art History*, London, Phaidon Press, 2013, p. 14.
34  Stephen Beasley, "Radical Nature", *Frieze* (Reviews), 1 October, 2009, www.frieze.com/article/radical-nature-and-architecture-changing-planet-1969–2009 (accessed 10 November 2020).
35  T.J. Demos, "The Politics of Sustainability: Art and Ecology", in Francesco Manacorda (ed.), *Radical Nature: Art and Architecture for a Changing Planet, 1969–2009*, Köln, Walther König, 2009, pp. 16–30. Original reference: Bruno Latour, "Why has Critique Run out of Steam? From Matters of Fact to Matters of Concern", *Critical Inquiry*, Winter, 2004, pp. 225–248.
36  Bruno Latour, *Down to Earth: Politics in the New Climatic Regime*, Hoboken, NJ, Wiley, 2018.
37  Ping Lin, Exhibition Guide, *Post-Nature – A Museum as an Ecosystem*, Taipei, Taipei Museum of Fine Arts, 2018, p. 15.
38  *Taipei Biennial 2020: Exhibition Overview* (video), https://www.youtube.com/watch?v=Ot8QHCikGXM (accessed 1 July 2021).
39  Ping Lin quoted in Sherry Hsiao, "Exhibition Explores Taiwan's Role in the 'Global South'", *Taipei Times*, 28 July, 2020, www.taipeitimes.com/News/taiwan/archives/2020/07/28/2003740686 (accessed 22 June 2021).
40  Bruno Latour, 7 October, 2019, www.bruno-latour.fr/node/812.html (accessed 1 June 2020).
41  "For all of the money we are spending, NASA should NOT be talking about going to the Moon – We did that 50 years ago. They should be focused on the much bigger things we are doing, including Mars (of which the Moon is a part), Defense and Science!" Donald Trump, @realDonaldTrump. Twitter, 7 June, 2019.
42  Martin Guinard and Bruno Latour (eds.), Exhibition Guide, *Post-Nature – A Museum as an Ecosystem*, Taipei, Taipei Museum of Fine Arts, 2018, p. 52.
43  *Climate Change 2021: The Physical Science Basis*, Intergovernmental Panel on Climate Change, 6 August, 2021, www.ipcc.ch/report/sixth-assessment-report-working-group-i/
44  Martin Guinard (video), www.youtube.com/watch?v=Ot8QHCikGXM (accessed 23 June 2021).
45  Naomi Rae, "To Explore the Impact of Climate Change on Culture, the Curators of the Taipei Biennial Transformed Their Venue Into a Planetarium", *Artnet* (News), 2 December, 2020, https://news.artnet.com/art-world/taipei-biennial-2020-1927945 (accessed 23 June 2021).
46  Rae, "To Explore the Impact".
47  See Chapter 1, p. 31, Chapter 3, p. 80.

# Bibliography

Altshuler, Bruce, *Biennials and Beyond – Exhibitions That Made Art History*, London, Phaidon Press, 2013.

Author unspecified, "2016 Taipei Biennial Announcement on e-flux by the Taipei Fine Arts Museum", 7 July, 2016. www.e-flux.com/announcements/52417/taipei-biennial-2016gestures-and-archives-of-the-present-genealogies-of-the-future/

Author unspecified, Preview, "Manif d'art 9, 2019". https://universes.art/en/manifdart/2019

Beasley, Stephen, "Radical Nature", *Frieze* (Reviews), 1 October, 2009. www.frieze.com/article/radical-nature-art-and-architecture-changing-planet-1969-2009.

Bourriaud, Nicolas (ed.), *Taipei Biennial 2014: The Great Acceleration*, Taipei, Taipei Fine Arts Museum, 2014.

Carrigan, Margaret, " 'Post-industrial' Biennale de Lyon to Examine Shifting Social and Economic Experience of the Region", *The Art Newspaper*, 11 September, 2019. www.theartnewspaper.com/preview/manufacturing-the-lyon-biennial

Chao, Jenifer and Panos Kompatsiaris, "Curating Climate Change: The Taipei Biennial as an Environmental Problem Solver", *Journal of Contemporary Chinese Art*, vol. 7, no. 1, pp. 7–26. https://doi.org/10.1386/jcca_00017_1

Demos, T.J., "The Politics of Sustainability: Art and Ecology", In Francesco Manacorda (ed.), *Radical Nature: Art and Architecture for a Changing Planet, 1969–2009*, Köln, Walther König, 2009, pp. 16–30.

Gourmel, Yoann et al. (eds.), Exhibition Guide, *When Water Comes Together with Other Water: 15th Lyon Biennale of Contemporary Art*, Lyon, Fage éditions, 2019.

Guinard, Martin and Bruno Latour (eds.), Exhibition Guide, *Post-Nature – A Museum as an Ecosystem*, Taipei, Taipei Museum of Fine Arts, 2018.

Horrigan, Michele, "Stigma Damages". https://michelehorrigan.com/app/uploads/2014/07/Stigma_Damages.pdf

Hsiao, Sherry, "Exhibition Explores Taiwan's Role in the Global South", *Taipei Times*, 28 July, 2020. www.taipeitimes.com/News/taiwan/archives/2020/07/28/2003740686

Hynan-Ratcliffe, Theo, "EVA International Phase 1: The Eye, The Voice", *Visual Artists Ireland*. https://visualartistsireland.com/eva-international-phase-1-the-eye-the-voice?fbclid=IwAR2MMvIPan3h7eW2CZ8jxva20rnTtZy18hgH33M5GvN4ndyVf9Gpx4gEShk

Latour, Bruno, *Down to Earth: Politics in the New Climatic Regime*, Hoboken, NJ, Wiley, 2018.

Latour, Bruno (website), 7 October, 2019. www.bruno-latour.fr/node/812.html

Lu, Pei-Yi, "Why Don't We Sing? Rethinking the Curatorial Mechanisms of the Taipei Biennial for the First Twenty Years (1996–2016)", *The Korean Society of Art Theories*, December, 2017, vol. 24, pp. 104–126.

Manacorda, Francesco and Mali Wu, "Post-Nature – A Museum as an Ecosystem: Curatorial Statement by Mali Wu and Francesco Mancorda", *Universes in Universe*, 2018. https://universes.art/en/taipei-biennial/2018/curatorial-text

Manacorda, Francesco and Mali Wu (eds.), Exhibition Guide, *Post-Nature – A Museum as an Ecosystem*, Taipei, Taipei Museum of Fine Arts, 2019.

Oxenius, Christian, "Interview with Matt Packer, Director and CEO of EVA International in Biennials in Times of COVID-19", *International Biennial Association*, 6 November, 2020. https://biennialassociation.org/biennials-in-times-of-COVID19-eva-international/

Packer, Matt, "Introduction, Phase 1 Programme, *2021 EVA International*". www.eva.ie/wp-content/uploads/2020/09/EVA_Phase_1_Programme_WEB-Version.pdf

Pownall, Augusta, "We don't have the Power to Stop our Extinction", *Dezeen*, 22 February, 2019. www.dezeen.com/2019/02/22/paola-antonelli-extinction-milan-triennale-broken-nature-exhibition/

Rae, Naomi, "To Explore the Impact of Climate Change on Culture, the Curators of the Taipei Biennial Transformed Their Venue Into a Planetarium", *Artnet* (News), 2 December, 2020. https://news.artnet.com/art-world/taipei-biennial-2020-1927945

Taipei Biennial 2020: Exhibition Overview (video), https://www.youtube.com/watch?v=Ot8QHCikGXM.

Thunberg, Greta, "Our House is on Fire", Speech 25 January, 2019. Published as 'Our House is on Fire': Greta Thunberg, 16, Urges Leaders to Act on Climate", *The Guardian*, 26 January, 2019. www.theguardian.com/environment/2019/jan/25/our-house-is-on-fire-greta-thunberg16-urges-leaders-to-act-on-climate

Trump, Donald, @realDonaldTrump, Twitter, 7 June, 2019.

Universes in Universe, Preview, "Manif d'art 9, 2019". https://universes.art/en/manifdart/2019

Various authors, *Climate Change 2021: The Physical Science Basis*, Intergovernmental Panel on Climate Change, 6 August, 2021. www.ipcc.ch/report/sixth-assessment-report-working-group-i/

# 3 Environment and Empowerment

## Biennales as Legacy Projects

With a license to usurp traditional exhibition paradigms, biennales have the potential to advance long-term social empowerment and environmental sustainability in the communities of artists, participants, and consumers with which they partner. As seen in the previous chapter, conceptual continuities from the 2018 to the 2020 edition of the Taipei Biennial charted the evolution of a biennale as an organisation committing, in the case of Taipei, to themes concerned with the ecological crisis and interdisciplinary, collaborative modes of working.

This chapter focuses on projects that further disrupt established biennale paradigms of exhibition-making by building on previous editions rather than wiping the slate clean on a biennial basis. It demonstrates the capacity of biennales to reframe themselves not as discrete entities reinvented from scratch every two years before fading into the cultural memory, but as building blocks from one exhibition to the next, taking care to harness the achievements and knowledge gained from previous editions as they strengthen and further realise the organisation's overarching vision with each manifestation.

A useful analogy for this more sustainable curatorial model can perhaps be made with the political system. Just as the government of the day is compelled to uphold the nation's constitution or legal framework, the curatorial team's decision-making around exhibition themes and anticipated outcomes would be informed by the organisation's greater aims. This model encourages challenge and experimentation, while minimising the risk of over-capitalising on resources being deployed to projects that fail to support the biennale's charter. It keeps the conceptual dialogue open from edition to edition, rather than shutting it down at the close of each biennale. This model also supports the evolution and growth of legacy projects initiated by individual artists and curators, such as Joseph Beuys' *7000 Oaks*.

Two major international biennales are examined as case studies in this chapter. The first is the 2020 Biennale of Sydney in Australia: artistic

DOI: 10.4324/9781003130574-4

director Brook Andrew brought to the fore the art of First Nations' cultures and elevated forms of audience engagement to the same level of importance as the exhibition itself. The second is the Echigo-Tsumari Triennale in Japan, which has for over 20 years built a legacy of permanent artworks across pristine tracts of countryside, working in collaboration with local residents. The premise of this chapter is that new, accumulative models of exhibition-making that map key organisational aims across multiple editions can more effectively than old biennale paradigms achieve impact and relevance in the context of contemporary issues such as the ecological crisis.

## 2020  Biennale of Sydney

Art and exhibitions are often the first to be pushed aside in times of crisis, dismissed as having little relevance in the solving of challenges to hand. Nevertheless, the 2020 Biennale of Sydney demonstrated how relevance to social concerns can be infused when the curator acts with genuine "care". With an incisively coherent and global perspective to entrenched problems such as environmental crises, human rights, and social inequality, the exhibition offered an intellectually and visually rich platform for engagement with some of the most burning issues of our time. While biennales cannot "cure" the world's disorders, underpinned by care and empathy this exhibition opened new dialogues with often overlooked actors on the cultural stage.

This dialogue was staged in the immediate aftermath of Australia's 2019–2020 bushfires that tragically revealed the substantial gap between global environmental ambitions and Australia's reckless failure to address them. The Biennale was set against the backdrop of the COVID-19 pandemic, which over the course of the exhibition period actively highlighted the deep divides between society's haves and have-nots.

Ten days into its programmed three months, the exhibition closed its doors in response to the pandemic. Subsequent to Australia's initially efficient handling of the virus, the Biennale was able to reopen after a three-month hiatus due to lockdowns, albeit without the raft of planned public programmes. Despite the interruption and cancellation of key programmes, the 2020 Biennale of Sydney, more than any of the previous 21 editions, demonstrated the capacity of art and exhibitions to move beyond being a passive reflection of the world to instead lead conversations on topics not being adequately addressed elsewhere. With a mandate for collaboration, education and new restorative relations with oppressed and marginalised communities, it demonstrated how exhibitions can not only be provocative, but catalysts for change.

Titled *NIRIN* – meaning "edge" in Wiradjuri, the Australian Aboriginal language of artistic director Brook Andrew's mother's people – the Biennale featured the work of artists from countries, cultures, and identities historically relegated to the periphery of major art exhibitions. These included an unprecedented number of First Nations and many LGBTQI artists, bringing to the exhibition forum experiences from around the globe that found resonance with one another on many levels. Much of the work was documentary in nature, like Andrew's own artistic practice which appeared throughout in the form of strategically placed *Powerful Objects*. It was an unabashedly scholarly approach, symbolised by the use of old-fashioned classroom clipboards displayed on the walls in place of standard museum labels.

From the start of his tenure as artistic director of the Biennale, Andrew was quick to clarify that he is not a curator.[1] His curatorial methodology as an artist was to collaborate with other First Nations artists, including from countries not previously represented in the almost 50-year-old Biennale of Sydney (since 1973) such as Nepal, Georgia, Afghanistan, Sudan, and Ecuador. As an artist- and First Nations-led exhibition, the selected and commissioned works explored cultural and personal experiences of dispossession and resistance, resulting in a strong sense of solidarity and strength shared between geographically diverse communities.

At the Art Gallery of New South Wales (AGNSW), for example, the exhibition took over an area of the gallery considered sacrosanct by traditionalists, as Andrew disrupted Eurocentric historical narratives with the voices of First Nations artists from Australia, New Zealand, Africa, and the United States. Works by New Zealand Maori artist Emily Karaka, Zimbabwean Mostaff Muchawaya, and Haitian Karim Bleus were dispersed among the 18th- and 19th-century Glovers, von Guérards, Streetons, and Mackennals, challenging those colonial narratives with alternative portrayals of identity and claims to sovereignty. Madagascan artist Joël Andrianomearisoa obscured some artworks from the collection with black veils as part of a radical curatorial intervention in the lofty Grand Courts, where historic European art is housed alongside AGNSW's collection of colonial and early 20th-century Australian painting and sculpture.

In a staged confrontation between white history and First Nations' experience, individual artists' voices were amplified by the setting up of dialogues within the gallery spaces. Creating cultural and chronological juxtaposition was an effective curatorial tool, not only between artworks in the gallery itself but between how selected works already presented at other biennales were contextualised differently here. American Arthur Jafa's *White Album*, a filmic collage exploring whiteness from a Black perspective, for example, was a highlight of the 2019 Venice Biennale, where it was shown in a specially built, discrete cinema space. It was so much more powerful at the Biennale of Sydney, placed in conversation with 19th-century European paintings and sculptures portraying stories of challenge, death, and disaster. It faced off directly with a life-sized bronze of a nude young man brandishing a shepherd's crook, dramatically threatening an unseen enemy above.[2] Created in very different epochs and societies, the proximity of the two works underpinned in each the coexistence in humankind of empathy and beauty, cruelty and violence.

Throughout the Biennale, connections such as this were teased out between ancient, historical and contemporary cultures. Andrew expanded this model of cross-cultural convergence to also consider parallels and intersections between cultural and natural ecosystems. By adopting a nonhierarchical, interdisciplinary approach, he also opened opportunities for the inclusion of projects, like those in the 2018 Taipei Biennale, that may not otherwise be considered "art" outside the context of an art exhibition. These projects had a deliberate and lasting impact as vehicles of knowledge transfer, some fostering a legacy that far outlives the inherent two-year cycle of a biennale. While this exhibition was not the first to offer long-term legacy projects, it differed from precedents in its intention to advance lasting change. Rather than producing artworks that then find a permanent or semi-permanent home, several projects in the 2020 Biennale of Sydney were devised as permanent interventions or behaviour-changing initiatives.

For example, very early in the planning, local artists Lucas Ihlein and Kim Williams were commissioned to facilitate a plastic-free Biennale of Sydney, as Ihlein had done for the MCA in 2010 (see Chapter 1). Andrew also invited Adrift Lab, an international team of scientific researchers, to exhibit their findings on marine pollution and its impact on the oceans and ocean wildlife. Like Ihlen and Williams in their resolution to eschew and educate about plastics of all kinds, the causal link between ocean litter and seabird mortality in our oceans is the catalyst for the research work undertaken by the interdisciplinary team. The three researchers, based in Tasmania, England, and Lord Howe Island off the east coast of Australia, displayed a myriad of discarded man-made objects found in the ocean. At their base in Lord Howe Island, the scientists comb through the found items of marine rubbish and perform autopsies on seabirds that have died by ingesting or becoming entangled in mostly plastic-based debris.

The positive legacy of a work such as this stems from its educational value. Processes of scientific research are not usually visible to lay audiences, who tend to only learn about it if the results are published and deemed newsworthy. The images of Adrift Lab's findings, projected and displayed over a series of 18 table surfaces arranged around the space, were confronting. Viewers were treated to recordings of birds of all types being

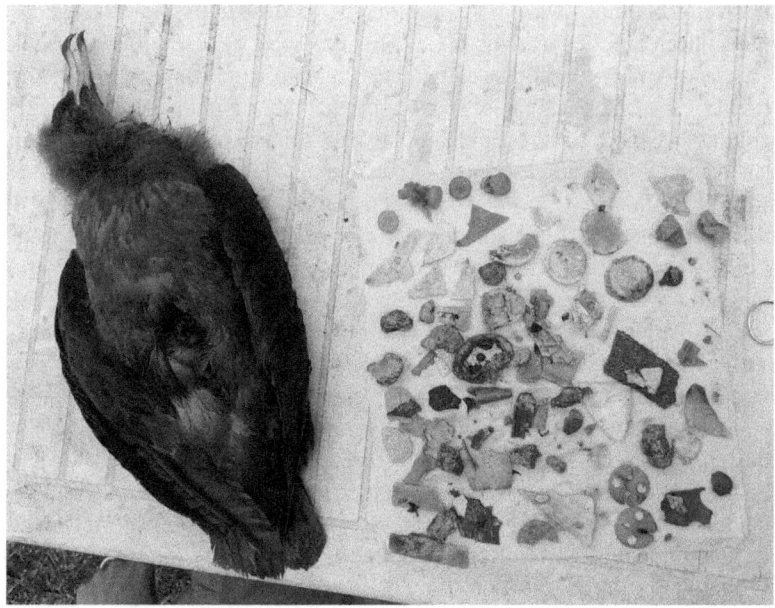

*Figure 3.1* Adrift Lab, *Stomach contents from a Flesh-footed shearwater*, from *Adrift Lab (Detached)*, 2020, 22nd Biennale of Sydney (2020), Cockatoo Island.

Photograph: Dr Ian Hutton.

dissected, the multitude of foreign objects found in their stomachs removed and displayed for close inspection. Species included the Bonin petrel and near-endangered Laysan albatross, both threatened by human pollution in the oceans. In addition to these disturbing films, found plastic objects such as Lego pieces, bottle tops, and straws were displayed. They included oversize items capable of suffocating large sea birds, such as garbage bags bearing the Qantas logo, presumably dropped from the sky. The hubris of human activity was laid out with shocking rawness, the installation's visual directness accessible and edifying. Here, as in the other key works that made a lasting impact, it was the artist-curator's decision to prioritise the raw data – the scientific research – over visual seduction that signals a new model of exhibition-making, one that is underpinned by the prioritisation of ecologically instructive content over aesthetic value.

Another project adopting an evidential, educative methodology was led by Australian artist Andrew Rewald. At the historic National Art School site in Sydney, Rewald created a garden in response to the climate crisis. The choice of plantings was, more specifically, influenced by the controversial (and since contested) 2014 book by Bruce Pascoe, *Dark Emu*. In the book, Pascoe attempts to debunk entrenched colonialist narratives around Australia's First Nations peoples by arguing that Aboriginal people were agriculturalists.[3] Based on research into the native plants that were nurtured and sustained by the Gadigal people of that area of the Eora Nation at the time, Rewald's *Alchemy Garden* explored the historical and potential future role of "ethnobotanicals" – plants that have cultural significance and are traditionally used to connect people and communities, shaping their understanding and experience of place. Methods of farming used by Gadigal people such as carbon sequestering, soil creation, and natural water management were reflected in the garden's focus on low-tech soil science strategies such as composting and water recycling.

The garden also demonstrated best practice sustainability in terms of its design, constructed with repurposed building materials and sited within a wicking-bed that drew water from a subterranean reservoir.[4] Workshops and demonstrations on ecologically sustainable food growth were curtailed due to the pandemic. Nevertheless, as a very visible, collaborative, and performative event, the creation of the garden and its subsequent lifecycle in the publicly accessible grounds of the National Art School (a convict built former prison) created an important legacy, educating by demonstration how native and non-native foods can be sustainably planted, cultivated, and consumed. The work also continued the Biennale's long-term commitment to presenting artworks in the public domain.[5]

Film-based work, including documentary footage, also played an important role in revealing parallels between human interactions with natural ecologies across different times and cultures. Of the Australian First Nations participation, this included documentary film footage drawn from the archive of the Australian Institute of Aboriginal and Torres Strait Islander Studies (AIATSIS). Exhibited at the Museum of Contemporary Art (MCA), the footage depicts the removal of sacred Dendroglyps (carved trees) in 1949 from ceremonial sites at the Kalimangl Bora Ground, a few hours' drive north of Sydney. The trees had been integral for thousands of years to the spiritual beliefs of the Gamilaraay people, and their removal by museum ethnologists was essentially a destruction of traditional religious structures. Central to the inclusion in the Biennale of the footage was a commitment to community consultation, which involved Brook Andrew visiting the town of Collarenebri to meet with high-school students, many of whom have familial connections to people of the Gamilaraay nation, the traditional custodians of the land. They watched the film footage together, the elders of the community attuned to

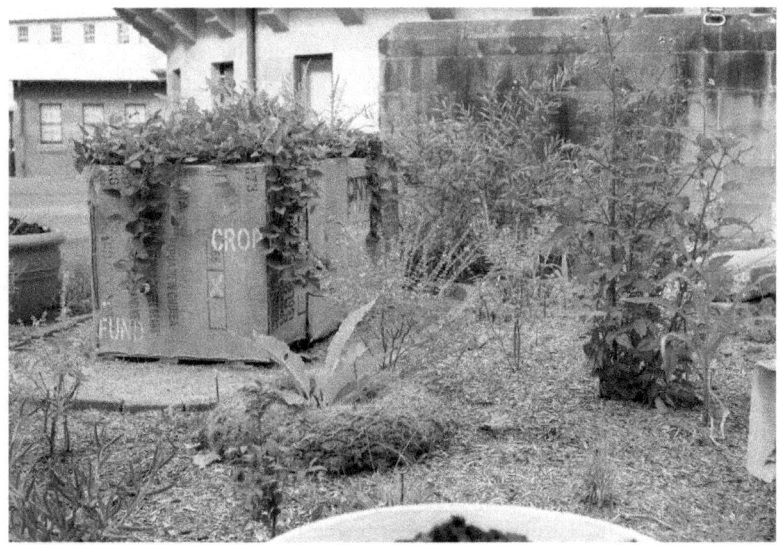

*Figure 3.2* Andrew Rewald, *Alchemy Garden*, 2019–2020. Installation view for the 22nd Biennale of Sydney (2020), National Art School.

Source: Courtesy of the artist.

Photograph: Alex Robinson.

the importance of the younger generation understanding these histories, hoping to inspire Gamilaraay and other Indigenous youth to stand up and make visible these often-hidden narratives, and to be proud of their cultural heritage. At the conclusion of the visit, the community gave permission for the film, *Dendroglyphs of the Kalimangl Bora Ground*, to screen at the MCA as part of the Biennale. In revealing this hidden narrative depicting the colonial destruction of culture and affording agency over its depiction and presentation, the legacy of this initiative is one of education as well as empowerment.

Another legacy project was commenced with the First Nations Dharug community in Western Sydney, who planned to lead a series of activations at the site of the infamous Blacktown Native Institution. This was a place where the "Stolen Generation" children who had been forcibly removed from their Aboriginal families were indoctrinated with European customs in the name of cultural assimilation. Symbolising dispossession, loss, and deep trauma, the land on which the Institution stood has been the site of healing and educational programmes in recent years. Again, the public programmes were cancelled due to the imposition of health restrictions. This did not, however, impact the Biennale's pledge to work closely in an ongoing capacity with the Australian Institute of Aboriginal and Torres Strait Islander Studies (AIATSIS) on a national programme of cultural renewal, to be continued in the 2022 edition of the Biennale and beyond.

The curatorial imperative to investigate and empower was also applied to the presentation of works by geographically and culturally diverse artists. Lawrence Abu Hamdan's *Once Removed*, for example, was like Jafa's also seen the previous year at the Venice Biennale. Here, it exemplified Andrew's goal to amplify voices of oppressed peoples through works that investigate analogous stories of ignored and concealed histories across cultures. Abu Hamdan's two-channel film tells the story of Lebanese historian Bassel Abi-Chahine, who believes himself to be the reincarnation of a 17-year-old soldier killed in the 1980s during the Lebanese Civil War. Abi-Chahine belongs to the ethnoreligious Druze faith, which incorporates elements of Islam, Christianity, Buddhism, and Hinduism, including a belief in reincarnation. Lebanese-British artist Abu Hamdan also grew up in a Lebanese Druze environment. The Turner Prize co-winner refers to himself as a "Private Ear", an audio detective capturing and sharing through his work recordings of victims and witnesses of civil unrest and injustice. His findings have been used as evidence in the UK Asylum and Immigration Tribunal and as advocacy for Amnesty International and other human rights organisations.

Invisibility was a recurring theme throughout the Biennale, applied to instances of cultural removal such as the case of the Dendroglyps, and finding comparable examples of erasure in other cultural histories, including the project by Mexican artist Theresa Margolles. Informed by the ongoing trauma of violent events and underpinned by collaborative, local research – a characteristic trait of Margolles's approach – the installation immersed viewers in a sensorial tribute to victims of gender-based violence, specifically the murder or disappearance of women in Mexico and Sydney. Working with students from the National Art School, the artist developed performative actions to collect the essence of each of the Australian crime sites by using water to absorb material from the ground. Inside a perimeter of red industrial curtains was a row of steaming iron plates onto which drops of the collected water fell, invoking the ongoing and visceral presence of trauma.

These works, among others, offered a global context and in turn a shared platform for gaining insight into works by local artists. Offering a sprinkling of artworks already familiar on the current biennale circuit is a tactic also adopted by the new wave of environmentally focused biennales. In order to retain their supporters and position in the international art world, biennales cannot risk alienating traditional biennale stakeholders – audiences, artists, and financiers. While still very much "on message" thematically, well-known and previously encountered artworks are a kind of lingua franca for biennale stalwarts: they infuse the exhibition with recognisable signifiers of membership to the international biennale circuit.

The mission to reveal sometimes hidden cultures was exemplified in the contribution of Australian First Nations such as Tony Albert. Visitors were able to immerse themselves in a timber sanctuary designed by Albert on Cockatoo Island, a 19th-century convict penal quality and the Biennale's most popular venue since 2008. Like the National Art School and site of the Blacktown Native Institution, the location is burdened by historical trauma, lending Albert's work added poignancy in terms of inter-cultural association. The interior of the structure was adorned with native flora, including papyrus which is the grass that Aboriginal desert communities use to make baskets. Suspended throughout the space were woven baskets handmade by over 30 artists from arts centres across the desert regions of Australia's Northern Territory, including Bula'bula Arts, Gapuwiyak Culture and Arts, Numbulwar Numburindi Arts, and the Tjanpi Desert Weavers. Tables and chairs encouraged visitors to stay awhile; people were offered the opportunity to write messages on hand-crafted paper imbued with the seeds of native plants, which they could then plant in pots provided.

Albert's participatory contribution to the Biennale, *Healing Land, Remembering Country*, was eye-opening for non-Indigenous city dwellers. Revealing the land as a source of sustenance and raw material, the project linked back to Rewald's garden, bringing a First Nations perspective to plants and their cultural uses. The work also acted as a vehicle of connection through reflection and seed planting. With Biennale guides on hand to discuss the cultural significance of the various plants and baskets, the project revealed the ongoing role of First Nations traditions in achieving cultural and environmental sustainability.

The 2020 Biennale of Sydney's foregrounding of art by First Nations artists and its initiation of long-term community projects are its greatest legacy. It was a line in the sand for curating contemporary art, rejecting the dominance of a Western art narrative to embrace cultural diversity as a premise and starting point, rather than as a token inclusion. Brook Andrew confirmed that it is issues – environmental, cultural, and racial – that are the driving force behind new curatorial values aiming for long-term impact over short-term appeal. Furthermore, this Biennale demonstrated that it is often artists who are taking the lead.

The Biennale's shift in curatorial direction was not an aberration. In late 2020, Colombian curator José Roca was announced as the curator of the 2022 Biennale of Sydney. It was a significant choice given Roca's track record as a curator who works closely with multidisciplinary cultural

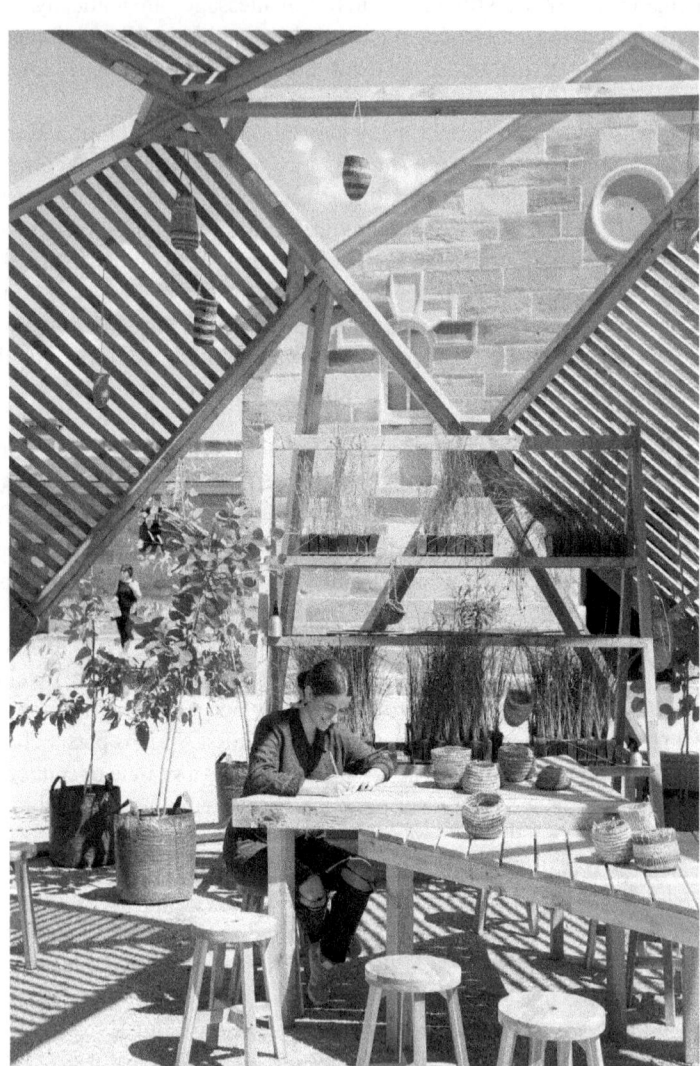

*Figure 3.3* Tony Albert, *Healing Land, Remembering Country*, 2020. Installation view for the 22nd Biennale of Sydney (2020), Cockatoo Island.

Source: Courtesy of the artist and Sullivan+Strumpf, Sydney.

Photograph: Zan Wimberley.

practitioners, including First Nations and local communities to devise and develop art projects that respond to challenges, typically environmental, in the real world. In a major shift for the Biennale of Sydney, Roca's commitment to meaningful rather than tokenistic collaboration was ratified with the simultaneous announcement of three Australian co-curators from diverse cultural backgrounds and boasting a complementary range of skills, knowledge and networks across Australia and the world.[6] Creatives included in *rivus* (which translates as "stream") are referred to as "participants" rather than "artists", reflecting the interdisciplinary nature of the event.

Building also on Brook Andrew's preferencing of Indigenous culture, the 2022 Biennale takes as its starting point the respect afforded natural environments in First Nations knowledge. Specifically, concerns around water as a resource that continues to be exploited in the face of imminent ecological disaster and widespread shortages is the thematic thread binding together installations by individuals and teams comprising visual artists, architects, designers, scientists, and local communities. The 2022 event also continues the 2020 commitment to sustainability. Recalling Demos' observation that "Exhibitions dedicated to sustainability are fundamentally contradictory", in 2021 the Biennale launched in collaboration with the British Council a "New and Sustainable Materials Challenge" to encourage Australian and UK startups, innovators, and manufacturers to incorporate sustainable non-polluting and recycled materials in artworks, installations, and exhibition sites.[7]

The thematic premise of the exhibition is not only timely but characteristic of Roca's practice. The 2022 curatorial team has posed questions that could be interpreted as far-fetched but have been embraced by the event's selected "participants": "Can a river sue over psychoactive sewage? Will oysters grow teeth in aquatic revenge? What do eels think? Are waves the ocean's desire?"[8] In addition to the arts organisations in Sydney that have historically hosted the Biennale, in 2022 – as the Biennale had or had intended to in 2020 – art projects are planned in temporary outdoor and public domain locations including in parklands along rivers and other bodies of water.

The 2022 Biennale's environmental thematic focus is adapted from the curatorial approach that underpins Roca's long-term directorship of FLORA ars+natura in Bogota, Colombia. The contemporary art organisation's mission is to "use intercultural exchange as a catalyst for social and cultural development".[9] This notion of the curator enabling through an art exhibition "shovel-ready" projects was echoed in Roca's rationale for the 2022 Biennale, for which he intends to deliver planned environmental projects under the imprimatur of the Biennale.[10] A reforestation project awaiting a creative lead, for example, could become a legacy Biennale project.

One former Biennale of Sydney legacy project highlighted by Roca in the 2022 edition is Joseph Beuys' *7000 Oaks: City Forestation Instead of City Administration*, an iteration of which was commissioned for the 1984 Biennale of Sydney just two years after Beuys launched the project at documenta in 1982. However, it was robbed of its legacy when a component of the work was accidentally removed, in circumstances similar to when art gallery cleaners mistakenly throw out art resembling trash.[11] Leading Australian artist Mike Parr, of a generation that well remembers the German environmental artist's contribution to Sydney, addressed the significance of and our amnesia around the "de-Beuysed" tree with a durational performance work in 2006.[12] Parr is among a handful of artists invited by Roca to exhibit a work related to Sydney's Beuys tree.

To mark the reopening in 2022 of the AGNSW's Sydney Modern extension along with the 40th anniversary of Beuys' original work and the 50th anniversary of the Goethe Institute's presence in Australia, Roca is also including two contemporary environmental art projects that speak directly to the Beuys work. The first by English duo Ackroyd & Harvey is grass portraits of Indigenous climate activists, a locally inspired theme related to their forest of living trees grown from and collectively titled *Beuys' Acorns* (2007). The second is *One Beat One Tree,* a digital interactive work by the late Belgian artist Naziha Mestaoui. It has real-world reforestation outcomes, inviting viewers to assume agency for the planting of trees. The 2022 Biennale's homage to Beuys both resuscitates and re-launches Australia's iteration of Beuys' most iconic environmental artwork.

In addition to its exhibition spaces, under Roca's directorship FLORA ars+natura accommodated FLORA Escuela, an "open school" for artists-in-residence designed to promote interaction and the sharing of knowledge with new audiences. Underpinning the programme was a proactive engagement with Indigenous groups aimed at fostering amongst artists and curators an increased sensitivity towards cultural diversity and ecology. Simply due to the infrastructure requirements and logistical challenges, an expanded field of curatorial practice is rarely utilised in more temporary exhibition structures such as biennales. Nevertheless, Roca has initiated a similarly broad range of multi-disciplinary inquiry in Sydney. Collected under the banner of The Waterhouse, it features for the duration of the Biennale a series of public programmes that include walking tours, workshops and schools programs .[13] There is cyclical appurtenant to Roca's project, given its focus on natural ecologies and the fact that the Biennale of Sydney came into being alongside the birth of land art.

From the perspective of curatorial continuity, 2022 Biennale of Sydney co-curator Hannah Donnelly has spoken about the beauty of the new curatorial team being able to "pick up the threads" to build on and expand projects initiated by their predecessor Brook Andrew.[14] Given that many of the 2020 public and legacy programmes were stymied by the pandemic, this generous and collaborative curatorial approach assumes a particularly significant role in ensuring the realisation of certain projects, including those planned with First Nations communities.

Another way of maintaining organisational aims and values is to minimise curatorial turnover. The rapid and regular change in artistic direction that is inherent to the traditional biennale model inhibits the success of legacy projects that require long-term planning, consultation, and collaboration, as well as ongoing activation and maintenance. In a recurrent exhibition setting where the curator is not replaced with each edition, however, a much more sustained continuity is achievable, offering real potential for a deeper, ongoing engagement with stakeholders including audiences. This has happened only very occasionally in major international biennales: the Biennale of Sydney secured Nick Waterlow as artistic director in 1979, 1986, and 1988, the only curator to be offered more than a single tenure, and the nascent Singapore Biennale contracted Japanese curator Fumio Nanjo as artistic director of both the inaugural 2006 and subsequent 2008 editions. The Echigo-Tsumari Art Triennale in Japan, unusually, has been under the same directorship for over 20 years, and is the curatorial trailblazer in fostering empowerment through art projects that respond to the needs of people and place over many years, unconstrained by the usual short term biennale planning cycle.

## Echigo-Tsumari Art Triennale

Since its inception in the year 2000, the Echigo-Tsumari Art Triennale (ETAT) has sought to revitalise rural communities and their custodianship of the unique natural environment. The Setouchi Triennale, launched a decade later in 2010, similarly aims to revitalise a rural area impacted by depopulation, re-imagining exhibition-making as a tool for social change in model that combines art, food, architecture, and nature. While both triennales work with their environments and communities in the conception and delivery of artworks, ETAT as the pioneering initiative with well-established community networks and long-running projects provides a more insightful case study for analysing the lasting impact of curatorial responses to rural decay.

The mountainous region of Echigo-Tsumari spans around 300 square miles of countryside and has a sparse population of just over 60,000, making it around half the size of London but with less than one percent of its population. It is located northwest of Tokyo (three hours travel time by train) and comprises six municipalities within the Niigata Prefecture. Traditionally a rich agricultural area best known for rice growing and to a lesser extent other crops, it boasts picturesque farming hamlets and hot springs, set amongst beech and cryptomeria forested mountainsides.

Depopulation has been accelerating for decades in Japan, including in the agricultural municipalities of Tokamachi and Tsunan where much of ETAT is staged. An ageing population coupled with a lack of opportunity for the younger generation results in the loss of around 1,000 people each year. Turning the tide is unlikely, especially by an art initiative, but ETAT is contributing to a revitalisation of local-based activities and labour, while generating interest in the potential of a post-agricultural relationship with the natural environments in people who if not for the Triennale would never otherwise have visited the region.

The population demographic of Echigo-Tsumari is similar to that throughout rural Japan: rice producers are small-scale farmers, mostly tending to just one or two hectares, and increasingly elderly (more than three quarters of rice farmers in Japan are past the age of retirement). Yet unlike rural areas in much of the world, Echigo-Tsumari boasts an abundance of fertile soils and natural water supplies, and a rich biodiversity not yet impacted by land clearing and chemicals. The loss of traditional rice farming, however, will inevitably lead to a much increased reliance throughout Japan and the world on commercially grown rice elsewhere by global biotech companies, resulting in land degradation, increased clearing and unsustainable demands on water supplies elsewhere in Japan and the world. Yet it is the cultural ecology within this rural area, rather than the land itself, that is in crisis.

Founder and director of ETAT Fram Kitagawa is from Niigata and, along with many of his peers as a youth, joined the exodus to the city in search of education and new employment opportunities. As part of the late 1960s and early 1970s protest generation, he was active in student politics, pursuing a progressive agenda of social equality at a time when the gaps between Japanese rich and poor, urban and rural, were quickly widening. After establishing Art Front Gallery in 1979, which remains a leading art institution in Tokyo, Kitagawa was drawn back to Niigata in the 1990s, firm in the belief that art could be deployed to halt rural decay and revitalise the economy and farming communities. With support from local politicians the "Art Necklace" was launched initially as a ten-year development project with the aim of establishing an arts festival and promoting the region's natural landscape and cultural identity. Over two decades later, its central platform, the Echigo-Tsumari Art Triennale, continues to thrive under Kitagawa's leadership, having carved a deservedly respected and unique position on the international biennale circuit since its launch in the year 2000.

From the beginning, the model adopted by ETAT was not only entirely site-specific but also underpinned by a commitment to work with and for the local communities, an innovative direction recognised as such by international commentators very early on:

> While the two Triennials held to date [2003] have seen participation by curators such as Okwui Enwezor, Apinan Poshyananda, Hou Hanru and Rosa Martinez on the advisory committee and artists such as Marina Abramovic, Ilya and Emilia Kabakov, Surasi Kusolwong, Cai Guo Qiang, Joseph Kosuth, Jimmie Durham, Kendall Geers and Maaria Wirkkala, all of whom figure on the global biennale circuits, the Echigo-Tsumari Art Triennial nevertheless is notably different from the usual global biennale norm. This difference, driven largely by Kitagawa's philosophy that the Triennial should generate a dialogue – between the rural and the urban, between Japan and the world and between generations – is demonstrated in his hybrid, inclusive curatorial approach.[15]

ETAT's mission statement emphasises nature, community, collaboration, and sustainability. Kitagawa's originating principle that continues to inform the activities of ETAT is a simple one: "human beings are part of nature". It manifests in temporary and permanent art and architecture, that, according to ETAT, encourage visitors to explore *satoyama* (countryside villages and mountains); foster cooperation between generations, regions, and social backgrounds; sustainably repurpose existing rural infrastructure such as empty homes and schools; and promote local produce and traditional ways of life including working with rather than against the forces of nature.[16]

Since it began, ETAT's focus has shifted from an emphasis on sculptural interventions in the landscape to the repurposing of abandoned buildings for permanent installations or art projects. Criticised by some for eschewing the tenets of socially engaged art practice, for the most part the art projects commissioned are standalone sculptures and, more interestingly, permanent installations by sometimes very high-profile international artists. The permanent installations comprise the Echigo-Tsumari Art Field, which is open to visitors much of every year. A number of them are designed to be activated during the summer months, with some artists having staged participatory events that educate visitors about the region's environmental particularities.

Australian artist Janet Laurence, for example, created *Elixir* (2005) as a permanent commission, transforming a small wooden storage house into a laboratory-like space reminiscent of an apothecary or miniature botanical museum. It is filled with glass jars and vials arranged on shelves and labelled, each one containing a medicinal plant from the region. Visitors

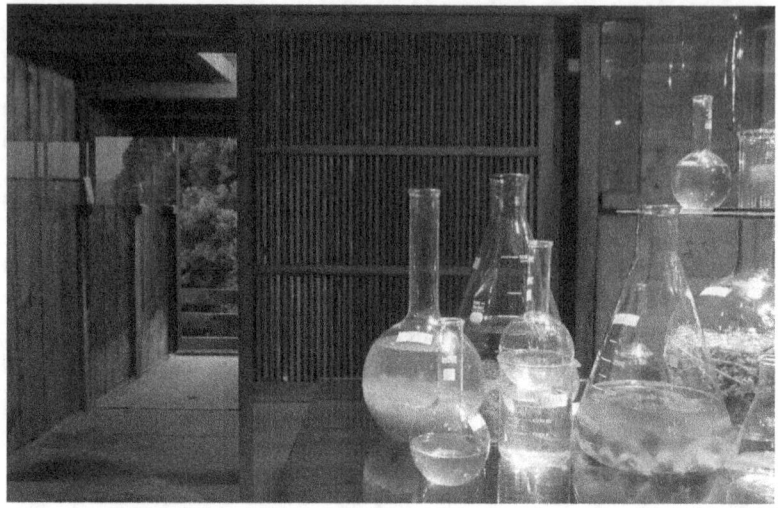

*Figure 3.4* Janet Laurence, *Elixir*, 2005 (detail), Echigo-Tsumari Art Field.
Source: Courtesy of the artist.
Photograph: Shiego Anzai.

enter through a medicinal garden where the herbs and plants are grown and once inside are offered an elixir, a healing potion mixed with the Japanese spirit shochu made from distilled rice. While Laurence's project does not directly contribute to the social and environmental issues that need addressing in Echigo-Tsumari, it was researched and created with the local community, and continues to provide insight to visitors about the region's botanical species and, when operating as a shot bar during the busy Triennial periods, has a reputation for cultivating excellent rice wine and local spirits.

Over its two decades, ETAT has articulated a dual role: to promote a passion for and in turn desire to preserve the region's precious natural environments and their inhabitants, and to revitalise the social and economic sustainability of the region with art and cultural tourism. The first aim is not unlike that of many other eco-tourism initiatives throughout the world and must balance conflicting aspirations to attract large numbers of visitors while minimising their impact on the natural ecosystems. By repurposing existing structures abandoned due to depopulation, ETAT largely succeeds in maintaining an extremely light environmental footprint. The second aim, of boosting the economy, conversely risks being judged by environmentalists as contradictory to the first, given that capitalist and environmentalist ideologies share little common ground.

Yet in relation to the history of international biennales, the undertaking to revitalise their local communities and economies with cultural tourism aligns with the same political imperatives that have been the catalyst for the launch of many international biennales, from Gwangju and Liverpool in the 1990s to Singapore and Kochi-Muziris in the 2000s. Other biennales have been established specifically to heal environments recovering from disaster, such as documenta in war-damaged Kassel (1955) through to Prospect in New Orleans initiated in response to the destruction wrought by Hurricane Katrina (2007). These underlying motivations are borne out by Kitagawa's original mission statement: while the first principle assumes the instrinsic link between humans and nature, the second principle is based on providing "A journey to explore Satoyama landscape following artworks as guiding lights", referring to visitors' routes that take them across the countryside to approximately 200 villages (including tiny hamlets with just a handful of residents), encountering over 200 artworks, and double that number when temporary works are commissioned for each Triennale.

Over the seven editions, art has been embedded into natural environments as well as into disused houses, schools, and other structures that have become surplus to need as the population declines. A permanent art museum, the Echigo-Tsumari Satoyama Museum of Contemporary Art, was established in 2003 to exhibit artworks from the collection. In 2015 ETAT launched the Isobe Yukihisa Memorial Echigo Tsumari Kiyotsu Soko Museum of Art (SoKo) in a renovated space that had been the gymnasium of the Kiyotsukyo Primary School. These ongoing initiatives continue to endow the region with a significant legacy both in the artworks themselves and in the potential for cultural tourism, additionally supported by Japan's government-led tourism industry.[17] ETAT differs entirely from other international biennales with its consistent commissioning of permanent artworks, their accumulation over the years creating a tangible and generative legacy.

Some discourse around ETAT questions the beneficial deliverables that such a mainstream event brings to a region facing rural decay and depopulation. An early analysis by Susanna Klien of collaborations between artists and communities from the first three editions (2000–2006) concluded that the local residents required more meaningful and autonomous involvement if social revitalisation was to be sustainable.[18] Ten years later, a slightly more favourable study led by Thekla Boven into the repurposing for art of 11 elementary schools in Tokamachi, the most densely populated municipality in the region, measured the level of positive impact for the community.[19] It found that despite the intention of ETAT to revitalise communities, there was an apparent uneven level of collaboration, with some of the major art projects being under-resourced and other more minor interventions being located in areas where the community is not only able but very willing to be more involved. The study concluded that this imbalance could be addressed by assigning more ambitious projects to better resourced areas, rather than risk failure with unrealistic expectations of a smaller, ageing community. It suggests that more research be undertaken at the front end of projects to ascertain not just the suitability of abandoned buildings, but for collaboration between artists and communities to assure the long-term sustainability of the work by matching its activation and maintenance requirements with community interest and capacity.

The former Higashikawa Elementary School, for example, was the first school to be transformed into an art destination, with Christian Boltanski and Jean Kalman commissioned in 2003 to create *The Last Class*. The installation was expanded upon over subsequent editions of the Triennale. Despite the installation being a "must see" for international ETAT visitors, it is remote, difficult to access via a country road, and has few local residents left to welcome visitors and invigilate, the hamlet's population having dropped to only a couple of dozen people.[20] When visiting during the off-season, snow sometimes has to be cleared in order to facilitate access.[21] Nevertheless, it is one of the highlights of a visit to the Echigo-Tsumari Art Field and as such contributes to the growth of cultural tourism in the area as a whole. The easily accessed Tobitari school, on the other hand, is relatively undervalued by ETAT despite a more active, younger community willing to participate in art initiatives. That cohort has instead turned ETAT and the Art Field's presence to their advantage with commercial activities aimed at art tourists, including the provision of rental accommodation, food and catering.

In terms of both community participation and sustainability, both the Klien and Boven research findings suggest that a more grassroots rather than top-down approach would likely provide greater long-term benefits for both people and cultural tourism. It is an issue long recognised and widely debated in curatorial discourse, particularly in the early 2000s by Claire Bishop and Grant Kester.[22] A recurring criticism is that in many community-based art projects it is precisely the community voice that is never heard, as curators seek to work with established artists who will impose a signature approach.

However, in the case of the artworks created for ETAT, "context-specific projects and artworks become meaningful outside the signifying context of the exhibition", a condition Claire Doherty ascribes to successful public art commissioned for exhibitions.[23] There are numerous examples at ETAT of this working well. One art project transforming local culture into a contemporary context of relevance to international biennale audiences, while retaining significance for the local community, for instance, is Japanese artist Chiharu Shiota's *House Memory* (2009). Shiota invited villagers to donate something from home, specifically something that they no longer used but also cannot bring themselves to discard. During a two-week stay in Echigo-Tsumari, the artist filled the inside of a vacant house from floor to ceiling with a web of black yarn. The villagers' objects are woven into the web, preserved and able to be visited as part of a permanent artwork.

As a curatorial conceit, sourcing contributions from people's homes has historical precedents that were also designed to build connections between the exhibiting organisation and local communities. The 1993 *Rendez-Vous* exhibition pioneered this model: organised by Jan Hoet and Bart de Baere, the citizens of Ghent in Belgium were invited to bring from home an object of personal value to the Municipal Museum for Contemporary Art (SMAK) for the exhibition. Four artists (Huang Yong Ping, Jimmie Durham, Henk Visch, and Ilya Kabakov) were commissioned to arrange the display of the borrowed objects within the museum in the context of their own practice, yet the subject of the exhibition was essentially the local people and their everyday lives.

Shiota's installation similarly reimagines vestiges of domestic interiors in Echigo-Tsumari. It literally "spins a story" of village life, casting old utensils, clothing, books, tools, and the deserted house itself into an interconnected web, a snapshot, or time capsule of sorts. It is a clever way of engaging with the local community, who feel a sense of ownership of the work having provided objects of historic or sentimental value, and those objects validate their continuing sense of connection to a particular place and culture.

Because of ETAT's dual mission to bring work by major artists to the region, there exists a curatorial tension between maintaining international art standards while respecting the original premise to meaningfully engage the people of Echigo-Tsumari. In some instances, well-known international artists such as Marina Abramovic and Boltanski have created immersive installations that appeal to biennale crowds due to the stature of the artist but are of less relevance to local populations. These provide a short-term (seasonal) boost to the local economy by attracting visitors, yet they are projects that lament the past, being nostalgic in spirit rather than forward-looking. The wistful tone is summed up in an installation by Ushioda Tomoko commissioned for the third Triennale, which reflects on a lifestyle long disappeared in a small village of the Shimonunokawa region. *The room of memory – people in Shimonunokawa* (2009) occupies a former general store, the only one in the area, which served also as a community gathering place. Today, its walls are covered in texts carved into wood. They are drawn from the memories of elderly and former inhabitants, an oral history gathered and transcribed by the artist. The fragments of text are reflections from a passing generation about their connection to the natural world and disappearing customs. It is a museum of times past, meaningful to the older members of the community but less so to younger people and visitors from elsewhere. Even as a non-Japanese-reading visitor, the overwhelming, almost visceral response to this mausoleum-like work is deep sadness. Two boats are beached in the centre of the room amidst the text-filled walls, their presence feeling more funereal than nautical. One is filled with objects from the past, and voices of the villagers emanate from the other, captured by the artist with hidden microphones. In terms of providing insight into the social history of the village, the immersive installation is insightful and very moving, assuming a museological role in the preservation of cultural memory.

Boltanski and Kalman's *The Last Class* (2006–2009) is similarly mournful. Situated in the gymnasium of the Higashikawa school, one component comprises a collection of pedestal fans atop low timber benches, with a forest of solitary golden light globes suspended above. Straw covering the floor is blown about gently by the fans while the sound of a heartbeat – Boltanski's own – emanates from the nearby science room. Evoking the absence through moving air, light, and sound of the active, curious beings that once occupied the space, the installation exudes a quasi-spiritual and melancholic feeling akin to bereavement. The installation was added to in 2009 in an upper level of the school: a series of acrylic coffins are displayed on a bed of white sheets, reminiscent of the snow that cloaks Echigo-Tsumari for months every year. In 2018 Boltanski added to *The Last Class* with *Le théâtre d'ombre*, a projection on the wall of the darkened classrooms shadows of skeletons, bats, and angels – creatures that mediate life and death.

In addition to his permanent installations at the Higashikawa school, Boltanski created temporary outdoor installations for ETAT, and at the time of his death in 2021 was preparing a work for the 2022 edition (postponed from 2021). The majority of his work at Echigo-Tsumari was created in collaboration with local residents, most notably *Les Linges* (2000), for which people contributed clothes, and *No Man's Land* (2012). Another work about absence and loss, the latter project resulted in an industrial-sized pile of used clothing, similar to Boltanski's Holocaust-invoking *Dispersion* created for London's Serpentine Gallery in 1995.

Given the late artist's obsession with death, the prominence of Boltanski's work in the depopulated setting of ETAT seems fitting on a conceptual level. In terms of revitalisation, his contribution lies both in the engagement with the people of Echigo-Tsumari as participants in the temporary works and caretakers of the permanent installations, and in the attraction of art tourists to the region. In a published tribute to the artist, ETAT organisers comment on the relationships forged between

Boltanski and the communities of Echigo-Tsumari.[24] It is an unusual strategy for biennales to commission a single artist to create new and build upon existing permanent artworks across multiple editions. Notwithstanding the fact that there is always a core group of leading artists who pop up in multiple biennales in different parts of the world at any one time, it is rare to see them included in the same biennale more than a handful of times, biennales being associated with the nurturing of new art, new artists, and new audiences. In the case of Boltanski and ETAT, repetition has achieved a sense of continuity and ownership, which is a valuable legacy not trialled in biennales elsewhere. The commissioning of Janet Laurence to create a new work for the 2022 Triennale is further evidence of the event's commitment to build on the legacies of key artists.

Less easy to assess is the long-term advantage of the Triennale in healing the ecological crisis. To be clear, however, this was never Kitagawa's ambition:

I have never had any intention of trying to do anything about the agriculture or the problems of the natural environment there. Getting involved in political matters can only put you on tenuous footing, and art doesn't have that kind of power in the first place. What I was thinking is that if the elderly men and women there want to die in the place where they have lived their lives, I would like to support that desire and help make their days as enjoyable as possible until that day comes if I can. And I also thought [about] what kind of give-and-take between the region and the urban centers could help this region survive.[25]

Just on a very practical level, quite aside from the theoretical debate, a crucial aspect to consider is ETAT's role not only in creating new opportunities but in maintaining existing infrastructure that would otherwise disappear from neglect. Since the year 2000 when ETAT began, an average of one school in the region each year has been closed due to depopulation. Around half of those have been "adopted" by ETAT, which assumes responsibility not solely for transforming the vacated buildings into art destinations but for their ongoing maintenance. Upkeep is intensive and incudes the prevention of deterioration especially following natural disasters – such as earthquakes in 2004 and 2007 – and the more consistent, laborious, and very dangerous task of removing snow build-up on rooftops during the harsh winter months. Structures not cleared of snow during winter are quickly subsumed and risk irreparable damage. In the winter of 2021, over two metres of snow fell in just one day, almost burying and risking the collapse of many art installations inside the picturesque old Minka houses dotted around the mountainous landscape. Sansho House, the largest former school building occupied by ETAT, which also provides accommodation for more than 4,000 visitors during the Triennale periods, required every able-bodied resident of Kotani village to dig it out from the snow coverage.[26]

Beyond a curatorial search-and-rescue approach to the architectural and human capital of the Echigo-Tsumari region, there are plenty of ETAT-initiated projects worthy of recognition for their ongoing community-building qualities. Hibino Katsuhiko's *Asatte Shinbunsha* (*Day After Tomorrow Newspaper Company*), for example, sees the daily production of a local newspaper by school students. Their news stories record the everyday lives of their village's tiny population, ensuring in the interests of community sustainability the noteworthiness of even the smallest of activities, achievements, and observations. Laurence's *Elixir* too, notwithstanding its labour-intensive requirements of bar staff during the summer months and snow shovelers over the winter, celebrates and shares knowledge about the unique qualities of the local fauna.

One of the most ambitious permanent commissions inspired by the natural environment is the Kiyotsu Gorge Tunnel renovation by Chinese architect and founder of MAD Architects Ma Yansong. Completed in 2018, it saw the transformation of a 750-metre pedestrian tunnel through rocky landscape.

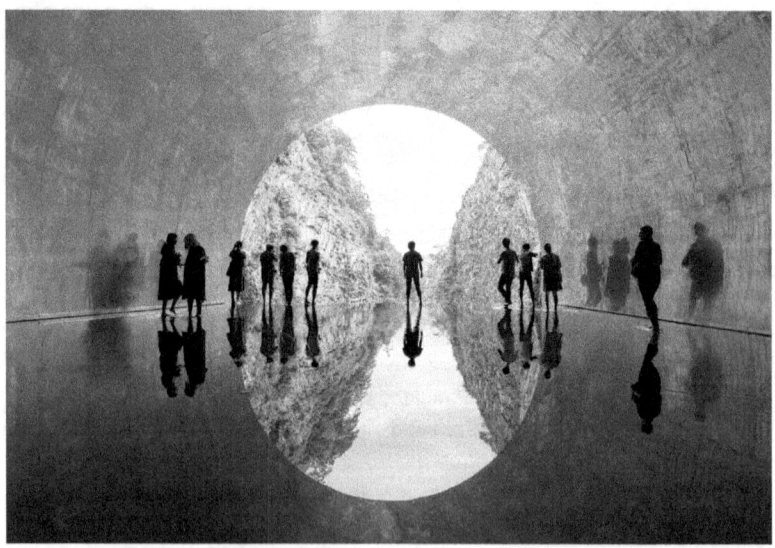

*Figure 3.5* Ma Yansong/MAD Architects, *Tunnel of Light*, 2018, Echigo-Tsumari Art Field.

Source: Courtesy of Echigo-Tsumari Art Triennale.

Photograph: Nakamura Osamu.

Affording panoramic views over one of Japan's most dramatic chasms, the materials used related to the five elements of nature – wood, earth, metal, fire, and water. MAD created five immersive installations along the route, including a room filled with distorting mirrors and a series of colour-changing lights, and a tunnel-like space in which water and mirrors are cleverly deployed to create an optical illusion that brings the natural world inside.[27]

Of the repurposed buildings, one of the most modest is Jean-Michel Aberola's tiny *Little Utopian House* (2003) designed as a gathering place for the farming hamlet's population of just ten people. It has a tall, semi-circular ceiling in a style that echoes the architectural rooflines in this region of heavy snowfall, and the entire interior is decorated with the French artist's characteristic wall paintings. A more ambitious work was created by Marina Abramovic for the inaugural Triennale in 2000. *Dream House* is an art installation that also provides overnight accommodation for visitors. Installed inside an old Minka house, the participatory work offers guests a choice of colour-coded pyjamas and rooms in which to sleep in coffin-like boxes serving as beds, and the following morning invites them to record their dreams in a journal.

Abramovic's provides a quirky alternative to James Turrell's ultra-luxe accommodation experience. *The House of Light* offers high-end Japanese-style accommodation, complete with tatami mat bedding, a natural spa pool and meals of local produce delivered by on-site chefs. A large sky window over the main living and sleeping area opens shortly before sunset and again before sunrise. Guests lie on their mats below, gazing at the framed view of the changing sky as it moves from blue to black and stars appear. At dawn, the sky window is set to re-open shortly before sunrise, allowing guests to wake up to the sight of the sky turning from black to blue (except during winter when they are likely to be awoken by snowflakes).[28] The experience affords cashed-up tourists a luxury experience of Echigo-Tsumari's magical natural beauty and culinary specialties, while providing employment for local people.

Besides remediating and repurposing building infrastructure, ETAT has been the catalyst for a range of sustainable development in the region, not exclusively in the arenas of art and environmental tourism. In doing so it has expanded the three-yearly exhibition model, commissioning art and architecture and staging special projects year round. Some are not related to art at all. In 2016, for example, a women's football team was initiated by the Triennale, a pioneering project titled Agriculture x Football. In the first year, there were only two players, both of whom moved to Echigo-Tsumari to help build the team. The arrangement was that they would receive professional coaching, build a team and play in regional competitions. In turn, the "farmer football team" members learn agricultural skills, enabling them to support themselves in life after football. The team has risen to prominence in the intervening years, winning the Niigata League regional competition in 2020 and attracting six new players to the programme in 2021.[29] They train on the sports ground of the decommissioned Nunagawa school in Tokamachi, prepared with new turf by local residents when Agriculture x Football was launched. The old infirmary has been renovated as the team's locker room and ETAT has commissioned site-specific art for each of the classrooms. The deserted school campus, once a pungent reminder of the town's youth exodus, has through the Triennale been reborn as a centre for art and community gathering.

Through their love of both football and the rich natural environments of the region, the FC Echigo-Tsumari players have quickly become major contributors to the establishment of a new generation of farmers. Some knew of Echigo-Tsumari and its plight through the Triennale and Art Field, and some had grandparents still living there. While football is an unlikely constituent of an international art event, this imaginative initiative by the Triennale has boosted the long-term sustainability of culture in the region, the local economy, and the land itself. Importantly, by diversifying its support for the region beyond art to also embrace sport, the

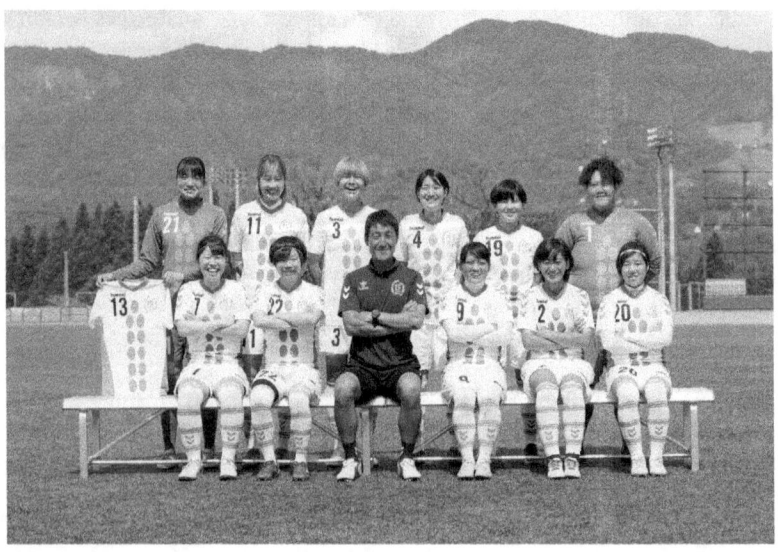

*Figure 3.6* Echigo-Tsumari FC, 2021.
Source: Courtesy of Echigo-Tsumari Art Triennale.
Photograph: Tanaka Satomi.

Triennale is sowing the seeds not only for continued cultural tourism but also for long-term population growth.

Art is not a silver bullet for rural decay, and ETAT can really only act as a buffer to and perhaps on a local level ameliorate some of the more dire outcomes of the world's ecological crises. Justin Jesty describes with alarming candour the conditions at Echigo-Tsumari:

> Villages are dying. Regions are dying. Ways of life are dying. Rural communities like the ones where ETAT is located are inefficient and unproductive. The urge to save them contradicts economic logic. . . . The challenge facing them is how to survive collectively in a world where the larger economic forces welcome their extinction.[30]

ETAT founder and director Kitagawa has demonstrated the ambition, passion, and means to contradict the economic logic by proposing and facilitating interventions that not only stave off rural extinction but seek to revalue human relationships with some of the world's most beautiful and precious natural environments. Kitagawa's position at the helm of the organisation is essentially that of artistic director, in addition to being chief administrator, fundraiser and creative force behind the organisation. Jesty also notes, however, that despite positioning himself and ETAT as advocating for a return to rural values and sustainable co-existence with nature, the art commissioned does not embrace the principles of participatory and socially engaged practice that offer new ways of relating to each other and to our environments, but rather the more traditional principles of monumental public artworks.

It is true that ETAT also differs from Western models of socially engaged, environmentally sustainable art projects in its retention of the idea of art as not necessarily performing a utilitarian function but as providing wonder and entertainment. ETAT is promoted as a family-friendly experience, the artworks dotted around the mountainous villages, paddy fields and wooded rural areas of Echigo-Tsumari creating a treasure trail of sorts. The journey of exploration is often punctuated during the summer months by temporary projects including for children, such as *Amazing Insects* in 2020, which through interactive learning explored the diversity of local insects in the Matsunoyama area. Although it is delivered and maintained in close collaboration with communities, whose continued existence and growth it strives to ensure, ETAT has to date resisted the rhetoric of socially engaged art, despite the simultaneity of the birth of "relational aesthetics" at the turn of the century. As Adrian Favell has noted, "Local Japanese art projects rarely frame themselves with the acutely theorized political self-consciousness standard to most contemporary art worldwide."[31] And unlike some more bespoke socially engaged art projects, ETAT is perceived not as an elitist or specialist art event but as being open and accessible to all.

Because they fall outside more recent models of programming and critical assessment, recurring rural festivals in Japan, which also include the Biwako Biennale and Setouchi and Oku-Noto triennales, have not featured highly in the global curatorial discourse. Another factor is that until recently the art commissioned for these regional initiatives is mostly incompatible with international biennale audiences' idea of Japanese culture. Contemporary Japanese art on the biennale circuit has historically favoured artforms that easily align with global perceptions of the more futuristic and populist aspects of Japanese culture, such as Pop and anime, tech and design, fashion and digital art. Ryoji Ikeda, Mariko Mori, Yasumasa Morimura, and Takashi Murakami, for example, have all dominated the representation of Japanese art in international art exhibitions including biennales for decades. Only recently has this begun to shift, with an alternative strand of practice such as Chiharu Shiota's immersive, labour-intensive installations of woven thread, Koki Tanaka's socially engaged interactions utilising natural and everyday objects, and Kawamata Tadashi's handmade constructions from timber which often involve collaboration with local residents, beginning to be recognised in major international fora (Shiota and Tanaka, for example, represented Japan at the Venice Biennale in 2015 and 2017 respectively). This evolving new and increasingly dominant strand of contemporary Japanese art is more closely affiliated with the sensibility of ETAT, in which the work of Shiota and Tanaka, among others, exemplifies its preferencing of lo-fi, collaborative, and experiential artworks. In this way, ETAT should be recognised as a pioneer not solely in curating the countryside but in fostering new and broader understandings of Japanese culture.

The global trend towards what David Suzuki describes as revaluing what has become de-valued should see an upturn in the international art world's critical engagement with ETAT.[32] To date, however, analyses of ETAT have focused on more measurable benefits to the current, diminishing communities. The interest has been in the Triennale's capacity to revitalise and expand social networks, and to boost the economy through cultural tourism that in turn can be a catalyst for homegrown tourism services such as food and accommodation.

To support his vision, Kitagawa has put in place a curatorial framework that borrows from the principles of site-specific public art, biennales, environmental activism, and, to a lesser extent as noted earlier, socially engaged practice. First, a large proportion of artists are already well-established in Japan or internationally, members of the "biennale club class". Second, selected artists are encouraged to visit and spend time in the region, getting to know the land and its (mostly elderly) people, and coordinating with ETAT's (mostly young) army of volunteers. Commissioned projects are physically site-specific and mostly conceptually relevant to the region, responding to the unique topography, climate, and cultural life of the region. In terms of alignment with socially engaged curatorial models, where possible works are created and maintained in collaboration with local people, a process facilitated primarily through the volunteers with the support of ETAT staff.

A key aspect distinguishing ETAT from other international biennale and outdoor art festivals, however, is the relationship with its audience. Embedded in its vision is a requirement for visitors to traverse the mountainous landscape, forests and paddy fields – by minibus, private car, bicycle, or even on foot. This takes time. While the artworks might be "accessible" in terms of their intellectual comprehension, physical access sometimes demands a purposefulness not usually required by biennale audiences. Many artworks are deliberately sited in out-of-the-way, difficult to access locations that take visitors deep into the countryside, often well off the beaten track.

Despite mostly resisting to date the opportunity to elevate the visitor experience from that of spectator, other than requiring more patience and sensible walking shoes, ETAT has opened up an otherwise little-known and inaccessible area of largely natural countryside to city dwellers and international art tourists. While "ETAT does not provide any concrete solutions to the structural problems that the Echigo-Tsumari region has grappled with", as Klien, one of ETAT's foremost critics noted in 2010, it provides

> a forum that helps to correct the growing disparity between various groups in Japanese society by asking visitors and involved actors to rethink the accepted paradigms of contemporary life, such as the urban lifestyle focused on convenience, effectiveness, and consumption, and re-emphasize the relations between man and nature, communication, and the importance of neglected ancient social practices.[33]

In the decade or more since Klien's analysis, ETAT's reputation and visitation have grown exponentially. In 2018, the event attracted 540,000 visitors from across Japan and the world, an extraordinarily high number given the remoteness of and challenges to accessing the various sites. Over half, or around a hundred of the rural hamlets in the region are now involved in hosting visiting ETAT artists. The participation of their ageing residents is not only building a sense of purpose and achievement in the residents of these mostly very small communities but also fostering engagement between artists, exhibition volunteers, and visitors from afar. As such, and in the instances where collaboration is meaningful and not tokenistic, there is tremendous reciprocal benefit to be had for both artworkers and villagers.

Kitagawa's curatorial approach does adopt a hierarchical Western model of curating and commissioning contemporary and public art, yet his resolute commitment first and foremost is as much to the art as it is to the Echigo-Tsumari region. As noted by Favell, "Kitagawa [is] not just bringing tourists to the area but transforming locals, visitors, and their relationship in the process. By any account, it is a remarkable vision of what art can be and do."[34] Another leading scholar of Japanese socially engaged and environmental art, Ewa Machotka (despite in the context of an article that finds fault with many aspects of ETAT), asserts, "Even if satoyama functions as a romantic trope that remains powerless in the face of extreme social and ecological crises . . . the affective potential of the art created for the ETAT remains undiminished."[35] The organisation's role in nurturing a sense of community between the custodians of the land and a younger generation of artists and other workers from very different, mostly urban backgrounds has been very successful.

While some have identified "a distinct whiff of political co-optation hovering around many of the art projects embraced as part of community rebuilding since the triple disasters of March 2011", the overall positive outcomes of ETAT over more than two decades cannot be disputed.[36] At a time of global ecological crisis, engendering a deep appreciation of natural ecosystems and the communities that have custodianship over them, by sharing precious and unique environments whether through art or some other means, plays an important role in deepening human understanding of and sense of urgency to advocate care for the natural world.

Further, by envisaging each edition not as a clean slate but as a building block, ETAT demonstrates how biennales can strengthen their position as stakeholders around ecological crises and sustainability. The consistency of ETAT's vision and thematic direction has ensured the organisation's accumulative legacy to the region. This is the model that has underpinned the success of ETAT, obviously advantaged by the 22-year tenure of its founding artistic director. Triennales come and go, but the organisation works closely within the community between each edition and welcomes visitors year-round to experience the growing number of permanent artworks and associated public and community programmes. At present ETAT is a unique model, but there are signs that other biennales are starting to envisage their exhibitions not as standalone editions but as chapters of a larger narrative.

# Notes

1 Author's interview with Brook Andrew, Sydney, 10 September, 2019.
2 *Retaliation*, 1878, by Charles Bell Birch (British: 1832–1893), Art Gallery of New South Wales collection.
3 Bruce Pascoe, *Dark Emu*, Broome, Magabala Books, 2014. The author's claim that traditionally Aboriginal people were agriculturalists was subsequently contested: see Peter Sutton and Keryn Walshe, *Farmers or Hunter-Gatherers? The 'Dark Emu' Debate*, Melbourne, Melbourne University Press, 2021.
4 For further information see *NIRIN* (exhibition catalogue), Sydney, Biennale of Sydney Ltd., 2020, p. 110.
5 The Biennale of Sydney's history of presenting works in the public domain was explored in an exhibition curated by the author and staged alongside the 2020 edition: Felicity Fenner (curator), *City Dialogue: Public Art Interventions + the Biennale of Sydney*, Sydney, Customs House, 2019–2021.
6 The 2022 Biennale of Sydney curatorium comprises: Anna Davis, curator at the Museum of Contemporary Art; Paschal Daantos Berry, Head of Learning and Participation at the Art Gallery of New South Wales; Hannah Donnelly, First Nations Programs, Information + Cultural Exchange (Parramatta, Western Sydney); and Talia Linz, curator at Artspace, Sydney.
7 T.J. Demos, "The Politics of Sustainability: Art and Ecology", in Francesco Manacorda (ed.), *Radical Nature: Art and Architecture for a Changing Planet, 1969–2009*, Köln, Walther König, 2009, pp. 16–30.
8 Media release, "Biennale of Sydney Announces 2022 Exhibition: *rīvus*", 13 April, 2021.
9 http://arteflora.org/programa/programa-publico/ (accessed 30 April 2020).
10 Conversation between Jose Roca and Felicity Fenner, Sydney, 3 May, 2021.
11 See Chapter 1 for a full discussion of *7000 Oaks* in Sydney.
12 Commissioned by the Art Gallery of NSW in 2006, Parr staged a durational performance in which he gilded with gold paint the stump of his congenitally deformed arm, and, dressed in a white bridal gown, circumvented the tree and adjacent area around the gallery for six days, until he collapsed.
13 Meeting with Jose Roca, Sydney, 15 March, 2021.
14 Hannah Donnelly, *Join us at the Forefront – in Conversation with Anne Loxley, Hannah Donnelly and Leanne Tobin*, Sydney, Information and Cultural Exchange (I.C.E.), 11 August, 2021 (attended by the author).
15 Sally Couacaud, "Echigo Tsumari", *Sonic Objects* (blog), 22 July, 2005, www.sonicobjects.com/index.php/2005/07/22/echigo_tsumari/ (accessed 1 July 2021).
16 www.echigo-tsumari.jp/en/about/ (accessed 7 July 2021).
17 Inbound tourism remains a pillar of former leader Shinzo Abe's 'Abenomics', despite being heavily criticised during the COVID-19 pandemic, www.japan.go.jp/abenomics/index.html (accessed 1 June 2021).
18 Susanna Klien, "Contemporary Art and Regional Revitalisation: Selected Artworks in the Echigo-Tsumari Art Triennial 2000–2006", *Japan Forum*, vol. 22, nos. 3–4, 2010, pp. 513–543, www.tandfonline.com/doi/abs/10.1080/09555803.2010.533641 (accessed 3 June 2021).

19  Thekla Boven et al., "Culture-led Reuse of Former Elementary Schools: A Survey of Echigo-Tsumari Art Triennial's Involvement in Tokamachi, Japan", *Journal of Asian Architecture and Building Engineering*, vol. 16, no. 1, 2017, pp. 61–66.

20  Boven et al., "Culture-led Reuse".

21  Author's visit, winter, 2010.

22  See Claire Bishop, "Antagonism and Relational Aesthetics", *October*, vol. 110, pp. 51–79; Grant Kester, *Conversation Pieces: Community + Communication in Modern Art*, Berkeley and Los Angeles, University of California Press, 2004, p. 172.

23  Claire Doherty, "Curating Wrong Places . . . Or Where Have All the Penguins Gone?" in Paul O'Neill (ed.), *Curating x 24*, Amsterdam, De Appel, 2007.

24  "In Memory of Christian Boltanski: 'Thank You, Christian'", *Echigo-Tsumari Art Field Official Web Magazine*, www.echigo-tsumari.jp/en/media/20210717_ christian-boltanski/ (accessed 20 July 2021).

25  "Presenter Interview. Art bringing Hope to Echigo-Tsumari: The Ongoing Journey of Fram Kitagawa", in *Performing Arts Network Japan*, The Japan Foundation, 18 August, 2009, https://performingarts.jp/E/pre_interview/0907/1.html (accessed 15 July 2021).

26  Minegishi Kairi, "In Order to Live Through in the Region with Heavy Snowfall" [sic], *Echigo-Tsumari Art Field Official Web Magazine*, 9 March, 2021, www. echigo-tsumari.jp/en/media/20210310_josetsu_winter/ (accessed 6 July 2021).

27  For a detailed description see Amy Frearson, "MAD Transforms Japanese Mountain Tunnel by Adding Mirrors, a Spa and a Lake", *Dezeen*, 8 August, 2018, www.dezeen.com/2018/08/08/kiyotsu-gorge-tunnel-japan-mad-echigo-tsumari-triennale-2018/

28  The author was awoken by snow instead of daylight during a Spring visit in 2010.

29  "Five Years on since establishment, FC Echigo-Tsumari Starts its New Chapter", *Thinking 21st Century Art in the World from Niigata: Echigo-Tsumari Art Field Official Web Magazine*, www.echigo-tsumari.jp/en/media/20210427_ fc2021kickoff/ (accessed 3 July 2021).

30  Justin Jesty, "Japan's Rural Art Festivals: The Echigo-Tsumari Paradigm", in Cameron Cartiere and Leon Tan (eds.), *The Routledge Companion to Art in the Public Realm*, Oxford, Routledge, 2020, p. 25.

31  Adrian Favell, "Introduction: What's Missing in the Field? in Socially Engaged Art in Japan: Mapping the Pioneers", *Field: Journal of Socially-Engaged Art Criticism*, no. 7, 2014, http://field-journal.com/issue-7/socially-engaged-art-in-japan-mapping-the-pioneers (accessed 9 July 2021).

32  David Suzuki, lecture attended by the author, Sydney Opera House, 30 November, 2010. See also David Suzuki, *The Legacy: An Elder's Vision for our Sustainable Future*, Sydney, Allen & Unwin, 2010.

33  Susanna Klien, "Collaboration or Confrontation? Local and Non-local Actors in the Echigo-Tsumari Art Triennial", *Contemporary Japan*, September 2010, pp. 158–159.

34  Favell, "Introduction".

35  Ewa Machotka, "Satoyama at the Echigo-Tsumari Art Triennale 2012", in Katarzyna J. Cwiertka and Ewa Machotka (eds.), *Consuming Life in Post-Bubble Japan: A Transdisciplinary Perspective*, Amsterdam, Amsterdam University Press, 2018, p. 226.

36  Favell, "Introduction".

# Bibliography

Author unspecified, Media release, "Biennale of Sydney Announces 2022 Exhibition: *rīvus*", 13 April, 2021.

Author unspecified, "Five Years on Since Establishment, FC Echigo-Tsumari Starts its New Chapter", *Thinking 21st century Art in the World from Niigata: Echigo-Tsumari Art Field Official Web Magazine*. www.echigo-tsumari.jp/en/media/20210427_fc2021kickoff/

Author unspecified, "In Memory of Christian Boltanski: 'Thank You, Christian'", *Echigo-Tsumari Art Field Official Web Magazine*. www.echigo-tsumari.jp/en/media/20210717_christian-boltanski/

Author unspecified, "Presenter Interview. Art bringing Hope to Echigo-Tsumari: The Ongoing Journey of Fram Kitagawa", In *Performing Arts Network Japan*, The Japan Foundation, 18 August, 2009. https://performingarts.jp/E/pre_interview/0907/1.html

Bishop, Claire, "Antagonism and Relational Aesthetics", *October*, vol. 110, Fall, 2004, pp. 51–79.

Boven, Thekla et al., "Culture-led Reuse of Former Elementary Schools: A Survey of Echigo-Tsumari Art Triennial's Involvement in Tokamachi, Japan", *Journal of Asian Architecture and Building Engineering*, vol. 16, no. 1, 2017, pp. 61–66.

Couacaud, Sally, "Echigo Tsumari", *Sonic Objects* (blog), 22 July, 2005. www.sonicobjects.com/index.php/2005/07/22/echigo_tsumari/

Demos, T.J., "The Politics of Sustainability: Art and Ecology", In Francesco Manacorda (ed.), *Radical Nature: Art and Architecture for a Changing Planet, 1969–2009*, Köln, Walther König, 2009.

Favell, Adrian, "Introduction: What's Missing in the Field? in Socially Engaged Art in Japan: Mapping the Pioneers", *Field: Journal of Socially-Engaged Art Criticism*, no. 7, 2014.

Frearson, Amy, "MAD transforms Japanese Mountain Tunnel by Adding Mirrors, a Spa and a Lake", *Dezeen*, 8 August, 2018. www.dezeen.com/2018/08/08/kiyotsu-gorge-tunnel-japan-mad-echigo-tsumari-triennale-2018/

Jesty, Justin, "Japan's Rural Art Festivals: The Echigo-Tsumari Paradigm", In Cameron Cartiere and Leon Tan (eds.), *The Routledge Companion to Art in the Public Realm*, Oxford, Routledge, 2020.

Kairi, Minegishi, "In Order to Live through in the Region with Heavy Snowfall" [sic], *Echigo-Tsumari Art Field Official Web Magazine*, 9 March, 2021. www.echigo-tsumari.jp/en/media/20210310_josetsu_winter/

Kester, Grant, *Conversation Pieces: Community + Communication in Modern Art*, Berkeley and Los Angeles, University of California Press, 2004.

Klien, Susanna, "Collaboration or Confrontation? Local and Non-local Actors in the Echigo-Tsumari Art Triennial", *Contemporary Japan*, September, 2010, pp. 158–159.

Klien, Susanna, "Contemporary Art and Regional Revitalisation: Selected Artworks in the Echigo-Tsumari Art Triennial 2000–2006", *Japan Forum*, vol. 22, nos.

3–4, 2010, pp. 513–543. www.tandfonline.com/doi/abs/10.1080/09555803.2010. 533641

Machotka, Ewa, "Satoyama at the Echigo-Tsumari Art Triennale 2012", In Katar-zyna J. Cwiertka and Ewa Machotka (eds.), *Consuming Life in Post-Bubble Japan: A Transdisciplinary Perspective*, Amsterdam, Amsterdam University Press, 2018.

Suzuki, David, *The Legacy: An Elder's Vision for our Sustainable Future*, Sydney, Allen & Unwin, 2010.

# Conclusion

When Mami Kataoka was appointed to lead the 21st edition of the Biennale of Sydney, she first of all set about researching the history of the exhibition. An unexpected find was the existence in Sydney of Joseph Beuys' *7000 Oaks*, one of the world's most iconic examples of environmental art. De-Beuysed and all but forgotten, Kataoka's discovery was the catalyst for its rescue and revival in 2022. If biennales are to make an impact as serious stakeholders in social issues of concern, they must look to curatorial models that accumulate rather than discard knowledge gained with each edition. As an analogy, if universities abandoned their research programmes on a bi-annual basis due to staff turnover, there would be a cyclical loss of expertise and scholarly networks that would in turn severely inhibit the creation of new knowledge.

Artists for generations have shown vision and leadership in addressing society's most wicked problems. Yet art by itself cannot change the world without a platform. International biennales are the most high-profile exhibition platforms of our times, their directors and curators entrusted with the power to amplify or overlook individual artists' voices. With power comes responsibility, one that is increasingly being felt by biennales in the face of climate change, as demonstrated here. Biennales also have the capacity to advance their organisation's key ecological aims by building on the research and knowledge accumulated over multiple editions.

The notion of curatorial "care" is being redefined by the biennales discussed here. In addition to their customary roles as protectors of artworks and advocates for artists, increasingly curators' duty of care is directed to environmental matters. Climate change and the resulting environmental damage were threatening the future of the planet long before the health pandemic captured world attention. In the possibly brief hiatus between COVID-19 and the next pandemic, climate change will again top the agenda as the world's most pressing challenge, its even more manifest presence

DOI: 10.4324/9781003130574-5

demanding an urgent rethinking of how we interact with the planet. The biennales examined here reveal how, beyond cultural tourism and political soft power, biennales can make a constructive contribution to debates and attitudes around a more environmentally sustainable future inhabitation of Earth.

What these examples also allude to is that the social demographic of contemporary art participants and audiences is changing. Large art exhibitions such as biennales have historically been considered exclusive, a perception based not solely on the financial wealth of their patrons but on those stakeholders' cultural capital. As biennales reach out to work with local communities, including those displaced by colonisation, globalisation, or climate change, cultural capital is being redefined to include new knowledges and skills, traditions and values. Biennales are opening the doors to new audiences, not by offering free entry to exhibitions (which does not address underlying feelings of cultural elitism), but by being interdisciplinary and paying attention to local issues and communities. The biennales discussed here are at the forefront of this reconstitution of cultural capital, harnessing alternative and collective approaches over the individualist preoccupations of star artists and curators.

The continuity between editions of the Echigo-Tsumari Art Triennale since 2000, in the Biennale of Sydney between 2020 and 2022 editions, and to a lesser degree across the 2018 and 2020 editions of the Taipei Biennial represents a shift in curatorial approaches aimed at increased empowerment – for both artists and local communities. Though still very much part of the international biennale network, on a local level they are chipping away at the cultural imperialism and exclusivity that have traditionally defined biennale exhibitions. Besides leading events such as these, some smaller and regional biennales are also moving away from the sole-authored, standalone biennale model to embrace collaborative exhibition-making and legacy building. Since 2008, Sweden's Borås International Sculpture Biennial, for example, has been demonstrating an ongoing commitment to fostering cultural legacy by commissioning outdoor sculptures every two years, many of which now belong to the city's permanent public art collection. And central to its 2021 re-branding as the Borås Art Biennial was a commitment to collective thinking and collaborative working. Testament to collectivity as an emerging force in biennales, the co-curators of the 2021 Biennial premised the exhibition on the idea that "Learning how to listen deeply to each other's experience is a way to build consciousness and a shared understanding of the world", the curators proposing that "new forms of collectivity" inform art and curatorial practice.[1] This trend towards collectivity is also occurring in other high-profile exhibitions: for example, the shortlisted Turner Prize artists in 2019 opted to split the prizemoney in the interests of promoting collectivity over competition, and for the 2021 Prize only artist collectives were shortlisted.

*Curating in a Time Ecological Crisis* shows how some biennales fore-shadowed in their response to an existential problem such as climate change the collaborative and community-based strategies implemented during the sudden readjustment of human life necessitated by the COVID-19 pandemic. During social isolation, globalism gave way to localism and there were unprecedented levels of cooperation between individuals and governments. As the book shows through case studies from very different parts of the world, these new collaborative ways of working with communities and across disciplines are ones fostered in recent biennales as they too address current challenges, in particular the ecological crisis and its impacts on so many aspects of our world.

Not included here, partly due to pandemic-induced postponements and travel restrictions but also because it is slightly tangential, is the recent phenomenon of artists being appointed as curators, including as biennale curators. The Kathmandu Triennale and Kochi-Muziris Biennale are two up-and-coming exhibitions experimenting with the new curatorial models discussed here: both the (postponed) 2020 editions have artists in key curatorial roles. Before the emergence of the curator as an independent exhibition maker, some of the most important exhibitions advancing new forms of art were organised by artists.[2] Similarly, artists have been curators since the late 1960s when contemporary art rode the revisionist waves of social change, though until recently the artist-as-curator model has rarely been implemented in the context of large international exhibitions such as biennales. Exceptions include the 2003 Venice Biennale for which curator Franceso Bonami invited artists, including Rirkrit Tiravanija, to co-curate exhibitions and a few large public exhibitions such as *Like a Moth to a Flame* held in 2017 at the newly launched Officine Grandi Riparazioni. It was co-curated by Liam Gillick, whose artistic practice, like Brook Andrew's, encompasses curatorial activity. Two anthologies, both titled *The Artist as Curator*, have been published on the topic, since 2015.[3] Curator Jens Hoffman's idea that *The Next documenta should be curated by an artist*, captured in a 2005 anthology of artist responses to the provocation, is finally being put to the test in 2022 with ruangrupa at the helm of the art world's premier event.[4] And ruangrupa, very much like the assembly collective of multidisciplinary creatives who won the UK's Turner Prize in 2015, are artists, not card-carrying curators.

Biennale exhibitions conceived as agents of change, whether directed by curators or artists, are nothing new. Twenty years ago, Okwui Enwezor's 2002 documenta built on his pioneering curatorial experiments of the 1990s to flip old paradigms in the context of the West's leading exhibition platform.[5] Other biennales have dispensed almost entirely with an exhibition, most famously the 28th São Paulo Biennial in 2008 which questioned the relevance of biennales by showcasing the empty spaces of the Oscar Niemeyer building in which the exhibition is usually staged.

However, deliberate strategies to achieve thematic momentum from one edition to the next, as discussed here in relation to the Echigo-Tsumari Art Triennial and recent biennales of Sydney and Taipei, denotes a new curatorial approach to biennales that preferences reiteration over renewal. This shift in curatorial thinking reveals that, being at the forefront of social change, art and biennales can lead the way through a "portal" to another world of possibility. Brook Andrew's curatorial approach to the 2020 Biennale of Sydney echoed the need to rise to this challenge, while also citing the original role of the curator to "care" and "cure":

> The Biennale demonstrates how artists have the power to resolve, heal, dismember and imagine futures of transformation for re-setting the world at a time of environmental catastrophe, conflict and reframing histories. Optimism from chaos drives artists in the Biennale to resolve the often hidden or ignored urgency surrounding contemporary life.[6]

We are at a crossroads where the opportunity has emerged for a curatorial reimagining of the biennale paradigm, and artists and curators are playing a pivotal role in the process. The 2022 documenta, curated by artists whose social and environmental values embody those discussed in this book, will be the first major post-pandemic test case. The question they proffered when appointed to the curatorial role in 2019 now seems extraordinarily prescient and even more pertinent in the light of COVID-19: "If documenta was launched in 1955 to heal war wounds, why shouldn't we focus documenta 15 on today's injuries?"[7]

It is not the intention here to argue for the replacement of a curatorial paradigm dominant since the 1990s by a prescribed new, leaner and greener version of exhibition-making. While each of the biennales here reveals the potential for thoughtfully curated exhibitions to lead the visual arts sector's response to social and environmental challenges, collectively they do not articulate a single curatorial template for universal application. While the focus of this book has been on exhibitions, biennales in particular, some curators have expanded their practice to incorporate even more immediate and potentially impactful responses to climate change. Inspired by the late artist Gustav Metzger's "auto-destructive" art that preferenced actions over objects, the Serpentine Galleries' ongoing, multiplatform *Back to Earth* programme of interdisciplinary events, podcasts, and publication (*140 Artists' Ideas for Planet Earth*, 2021) is testament for example, to the sense of urgency and level of frustration over the failure of political leaders to address ecological crises.

Just as the old biennale culture embraced the structures of capitalist globalisation, and is becoming less relevant as the negative impacts of globalisation are accelerating environmental damage, it would seem foolhardy to propose a fixed new curatorial model that embraces the tenets of post-globalisation, as that too will shift and evolve as we address the planet's future sustainability. Instead, an even more agile post-paradigm format is proposed by the biennales discussed here, where individual biennales and their stewards reinvent the curatorial model in response to local conditions impacted by global crises while building on knowledge accumulated along the way.

Though not a formulated model, the beginnings of a toolkit for ensuring meaningfulness in a time of ecological crisis have been identified among these biennales. The tools include commissioning artists to work with environmental scientists and enabling them to interpret scientific data; fostering multidisciplinary teams with a diverse range of skills and knowledge; involving the local community as participants and/or producers; listening to and foregrounding the voices of First Nations and other cultures previously overlooked in international curatorial platforms such as biennales; commissioning legacy projects that will continue to contribute to the social and environmental sustainability of a place; self-monitoring the exhibition's carbon footprint; ensuring local artistic production and thematic relevance; embedding public programme as central to the curatorial rationale; and, as an overarching organisational direction, conceiving of individual biennales as building blocks rather than standalone exhibitions.

The biennales that have most successfully embraced scientific fact and research into the exhibitions have buried it either within artworks themselves, for example in interdisciplinary projects between artists and scientists, or as parts of a narrative that blend seamlessly with and enhance the dialogue between artworks. If curators are going to guide people along the path of intelligence gathering forged by their artists, raw, sometimes scary data needs to be camouflaged – like green vegetables in the meals of children – within the overarching visual offering, as it is more readily digested when wrapped in the kinds of aesthetic joy and speculative wonder traditionally associated with major art exhibitions.

These strategies, among others yet to be formulated by emerging and future curators, are key to the ongoing relevance of biennales. In the meantime, as rejoinders to environmental challenges, set against the backdrop of widening divisions between haves and have-nots and a yearning for more equal and sustainable ways of inhabiting Earth, the biennales discussed here are cultural first-responders to many of the contemporary crises we face.

As the extent of the COVID-19 pandemic became apparent, writer Arundhati Roy, in an article for the London's *Financial Times*, painted a dismal portrait of the pandemic in her home country of India. Despite its confrontational content, her tone was optimistic. Taking a step back to assess the bigger picture, Roy proposed that the pandemic be embraced as a portal to a relationship with the world that is changed for the better:

> Whatever it is, coronavirus has made the mighty kneel and brought the world to a halt like nothing else could. Our minds are still racing back and forth, longing for a return to "normality", trying to stitch our future to our past and refusing to acknowledge the rupture. But the rupture exists. And in the midst of this terrible despair, it offers us a chance to rethink the doomsday machine we have built for ourselves. Nothing could be worse than a return to normality. Historically, pandemics have forced humans to break with the past and imagine their world anew. This one is no different. It is a portal, a gateway between one world and the next. We can choose to walk through it, dragging the carcasses of our prejudice and hatred, our avarice, our data banks and dead ideas, our dead rivers and smoky skies behind us. Or we can walk through lightly, with little luggage, ready to imagine another world. And ready to fight for it.[8]

The media release in mid-2021 confirming that Kassel would forge ahead with documenta 15 in 2022, despite known and unknowable challenges posed by the pandemic, avoided the usual hype associated with biennale announcements. It was measured yet optimistic, realistic, and not averse to risk-taking. Dr Sabine Schorman, director of documenta and its host institution the Museum Fridericianum, stated: "We can achieve a great deal if we move forward courageously and allow this documenta to assert itself amid a situation of ongoing uncertainty. I see an opportunity here for a new approach to sustainability in the arts and culture sector." In addition to confirming government indemnity for loss of revenue, the organising committee declared that "more important than aiming for new attendance records, the goal is to send a signal of hope emanating from culture".[9]

Documenta 15 is conceived around the concept of "lumbung", the rural Indonesian practice of storing the harvest in a communal rice barn to be shared and used for the common good. Viewed through Roy's vision of a portal, curator ruangrupa's stated intention ensure relevance to the times we are living in promises to adopt some of the proactive curatorial models explored by the recent biennales discussed in this book. While not wanting to assign full responsibility to ruangrupa – who are already making history as flagbearers of the Global South charged with curating the leading event of contemporary art in the West – the attainment of relevance to the times they aim for will validate the long-standing curatorial premise of the Echigo-Tsumari Art Triennale and the more recent propositions of the Limerick, Lyon, Taipei and Sydney biennales, and inspire curatorial change for good. The 1980s and 1990s witnessed an exponential shift in power for curators, from carers to cultural gatekeepers, philosophers, scholars, and creative agents in their own right. When applied to contemporary art and exhibitions, Arundhati Roy's "rupture" has manifested as an imperative to be relevant, prompting new curatorial approaches to address the ecological crisis. If curatorial practice and its outputs, of which major international biennales are the most impactful, are to maintain relevance in these challenging times, they must be open and adaptive, attuned to the environmental and social agendas of their artists while serving the needs of societies looking to art not just for inspiration but for direction.

## Notes

1 Ulrika Flink and Amanprit Sandhu, "Curatorial Text", in *Deep Listening for Longing*, Borås Art Biennial, www.borasartbiennial.se/the-curators-text (accessed 9 September 2021).
2 Bruce Altshuler, "Introduction", in *Biennials and Beyond – Exhibitions That Made Art History*, London, Phaidon Press, 2013, p. 11.
3 Celina Jeffrey (ed.), *The Artist as Curator*, Bristol, Intellect and Chicago, The University of Chicago Press, 2015; Elena Filipovic (ed.), *The Artist as Curator*, London, Koenig Books and Milan, Mouse Publishing, 2017.
4 Jens Hoffman, *The Next Documenta Should be Curated by an Artist*, Frankfurt, Revolver, 2005.
5 Enwezor's key curatorial breakthroughs prior to documenta were *In/sight* (Guggenheim Museum, New York, 1996) and as artistic director of the 2nd Johannesburg Biennale (1996–1997).
6 Brook Andrew, www.biennaleofsydney.art/archive/22nd-biennale-sydney-nirin/ (accessed 8 March 2020).
7 "Artist Collective Ruangrupa to Curate documenta 15", *Artforum*, 22 February, 2019, www.artforum.com/news/artist-collective-ruangrupa-to-curate-documenta-15-78758 (accessed 1 March 2020).
8 Arundhati Roy, "The Pandemic is a Portal", *Financial Times*, 4 April, 2020, www.ft.com/content/10d8f5e8-74eb-11ea-95fe-fcd274e920ca (accessed 4 April 2020).
9 Media release, 21 July, 2021, https://documenta-fifteen.de/en/news/documenta-committees-decide-documenta-fifteen-is-to-take-place-as-planned-in-2022/ (accessed 21 July 2021).

## Bibliography

Altshuler, Bruce, *Biennials and Beyond – Exhibitions That Made Art History*, London, Phaidon Press, 2013.

Andrew, Brook. www.biennaleofsydney.art/archive/22nd-biennale-sydney-nirin/

Author unspecified, "Artist Collective Ruangrupa to Curate documenta 15", *Artforum*, 22 February, 2019. www.artforum.com/news/artist-collective-ruangrupa-to-curate-documenta-15-78758

Author unspecified, "Media Release", 21 July, 2021. https://documenta-fifteen.de/en/news/documenta-committees-decide-documenta-fifteen-is-to-take-place-as-planned-in-2022/

Flink, Ulrika and Amanprit Sandhu, "Curatorial Text", In *Deep Listening for Longing*, Borås Art Biennial. www.borasartbiennial.se/the-curators-text

Hoffman, Jens, *The Next Documenta Should Be Curated by an Artist*, Frankfurt, Revolver, 2005.

Roy, Arundhati, "The Pandemic is a Portal", *Financial Times*, 4 April, 2020. www.ft.com/content/10d8f5e8-74eb-11ea-95fe-fcd274e920ca

# Index

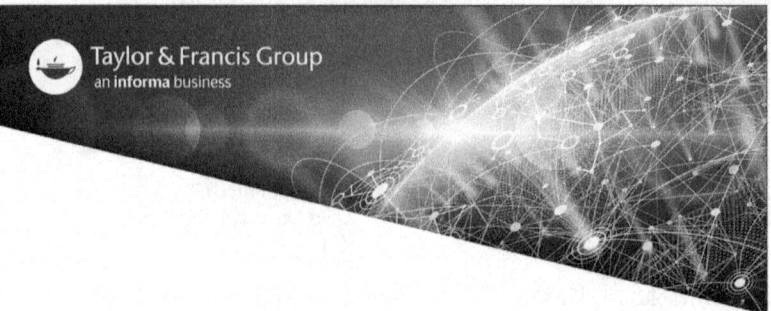
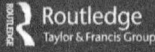
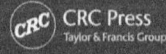

For Product Safety Concerns and Information please contact our EU
representative GPSR@taylorandfrancis.com
Taylor & Francis Verlag GmbH, Kaufingerstraße 24, 80331 München, Germany